IN THE COMPANY OF HEROES

IN THE COMPANY OF HEROES

The Inspiring Stories of Medal of Honor Recipients from America's Longest Wars in Afghanistan and Iraq

James Kitfield

CENTER
STREET

NEW YORK • NASHVILLE

Center Street
Hachette Book Group
1290 Avenue of the Americas, New York, NY 10104
centerstreet.com
twitter.com/centerstreet

First Edition: August 2021

Center Street is a division of Hachette Book Group, Inc. The Center Street name and logo are trademarks of Hachette Book Group, Inc.

The publisher is not responsible for websites (or their content) that are not owned by the publisher.

Library of Congress Cataloging-in-Publication Data has been applied for.

ISBNs: 978-1-5460-8579-9 (hardcover), 978-1-5460-8580-5 (ebook)

Printed in the United States of America

LSC-C

Printing 1, 2021

Dedicated to the uniformed volunteers who answered the call and fought their nation's longest wars after the September 11, 2001, terrorist attacks:
"The New Greatest Generation."

Contents

Introduction

On an unseasonably warm evening in mid-September 2018, a crowd of Naval Academy midshipmen in starched uniforms poured through the entryway of Dahlgren Hall. The cavernous Beaux-Arts structure was buzzing with excitement. The young midshipmen had been promised a Friday night of celebration and celebrity, with "Patriot Awards" to be given to Secretary of Defense James Mattis, Fox News anchor Chris Wallace, Senator Susan Collins of Maine, and former *Tonight Show* comedian Jay Leno. Yet the patriots many of the midshipmen most wanted to meet on September 15, 2018, were not celebrities or politicians, but rather members of the world's most exclusive fraternity.

Admission into the Congressional Medal of Honor Society cannot be purchased with any currency other than valor. Of the only seventy-two then-living recipients of the Medal of Honor—the nation's highest military award for bravery in combat "above and beyond the call of duty"—fully forty-four attended the annual meeting in Annapolis, the society's first-ever event at the service academy. Each of them had emerged through a painstaking process that begins with a recommendation from their chain of command or Congress, is subjected to months of intense scrutiny and investigation by a Decorations Board and must be approved by the Pentagon's head of Manpower and Reserve Affairs, the chief of staff of their particular armed service, the secretary of defense, and ultimately the president of the United States.

Besides the Patriot Awards dinner, the Medal of Honor Society's four-day convention included a town hall forum and autograph session with the public, a private lunch with Naval Academy midshipmen, a parade ground review of the academy's marching brigade, and a Navy football game. At every stop and venue, crowds gathered close to these heroes to be reminded of something essential about the American character. The extraordinary qualities and principles they embody are often lost in our celebrity culture and in the self-absorption of social media, or they are discounted in an endless news cycle driven by sensational headlines and clickbait. Yet these men are nevertheless a true reflection of the parents and communities across the nation that raised them, and especially of the many nameless men and women in uniform who served by their sides and watched their backs. Their stories recall the broad sweep of history that has seen generation after generation of Americans called to duty during times of war.

That trumpet sounded even before President Abraham Lincoln first established the Congressional Medal of Honor in 1862 to recognize "such noncommissioned officers and privates as shall most distinguish themselves by their gallantry in action, and other soldier-like qualities during the present insurrection." In 1863 the medal became a permanent military decoration available to all in uniform, including commissioned officers. That expansion came in time to honor Colonel Joshua Lawrence Chamberlain. On July 2, 1863, during the Battle of Gettysburg, Chamberlain defended the left flank of the Union army from repeated Confederate attacks on Little Round Top. When his 20th Maine was decimated by casualties and nearly out of ammunition, Chamberlain ordered a bayonet charge down the mountain that broke the Confederate lines and helped secure victory in the decisive battle of the Civil War.

So it has been with the other 3,526 Medals of Honor awarded since it was established, a constellation of heroism delineating a nation born of high ideals, yet defended and sustained only through martial will and bloody sacrifice. The arc of America's ascendance from a fledgling democracy ultimately to an unrivaled global superpower is also revealed in that accounting.

There were 1,523 Medals of Honor awarded during the war to preserve the Union, and 426 for the Indian campaigns as the country expanded westward in the name of Manifest Destiny. The colonial-era wars of the late 1800s and early 1900s (the Spanish-American War, Philippines War, Samoan campaign, Chinese Boxer Rebellion, and Haitian and Dominican campaigns) produced 268 Medal of Honor recipients. The U.S. entry into World War I eventually led to 126 Medals of Honor being awarded, notably to include Sergeant Alvin York, a freckle-faced Tennessee mountaineer and would-be conscientious objector who became a legend for his actions in the

Argonne Forest during the final offensive of the war. York was credited with killing 25 German soldiers, silencing 35 enemy machine guns, and single-handedly capturing 132 German prisoners.

The Second World War fitted the United States for its superpower uniform, and the fighting in the Atlantic and Pacific theaters produced no fewer than 472 Medal of Honor recipients. They notably included Audie Murphy, the hard-scrabble son of sharecroppers who lied in order to enlist in the Army at the age of sixteen, and at nineteen was credited with holding off an entire company of German soldiers. Murphy killed or wounded an estimated 50 German troops before suffering a severe leg wound, and then led a counterattack that decided the battle. Murphy would go on to become one of the most decorated soldiers of the war as well as a Hollywood actor and celebrity, though he never fully recovered from the post-traumatic stress disorder (PTSD) that plagues so many combat veterans.

Of the rapidly dwindling number of World War II Medal of Honor recipients, Hershel "Woody" Williams made it to the Annapolis convention in September 2018. The youngest of eleven children and raised on a dairy farm in West Virginia, Williams was rejected on his first attempt to enlist in the Marine Corps in 1942 because he was too short. Armed with a flamethrower, he would later single-handedly clear a network of reinforced Japanese pillboxes and machine-gun emplacements during the battle for Iwo Jima. He stood tall in receiving the Medal of Honor from President Harry S. Truman.

The Korean War that foreshadowed the long, twilight struggle of the Cold War between democracy and communism produced 145 Medal of Honor recipients. They included Japanese American Hiroshi "Hershey" Miyamura, who also attended the Annapolis reunion. Miyamura's wife had been incarcerated in an internment camp in the United States while he fought with the all-Nisei 100th Infantry Battalion in World War II. During the Korean War, Miyamura killed more than 50 Chinese troops, some in hand-to-hand combat, to give his fellow soldiers time to retreat and avoid being overrun or captured. He was wounded and spent the next twenty-eight months in a North Korean prisoner of war camp, later receiving the Medal of Honor from President Dwight D. Eisenhower.

And there in Annapolis was Bruce Crandall, a former All-American baseball player in high school in Olympia, Washington, who in 1965 served as an Army helicopter pilot in Vietnam. After the Army's 7th Cavalry Regiment was ambushed and surrounded in the Ia Drang Valley, some medivac crews refused to fly into the intensely hot landing zone. So Crandall continuously flew unarmed Huey helicopters on twenty-two missions into the teeth of the enemy fire, ruining many helicopters but managing to evacuate 70 wounded soldiers and deposit the ammunition that allowed the 7th Calvary to survive the night. He received the Medal of Honor in 2007 from President George W. Bush.

Few who talked to these rare individuals and heard their stories in Annapolis in September 2018 walked away uninspired. Theirs are stories of never surrendering despite harrowing odds, of facing death and finding the courage and faith not to be cowed, of wearing their scars like badges of honor. There is wisdom and warrior fierceness in these narratives, but also acts of profound tenderness. The common theme running throughout is men caught in a brush with eternity, and choosing to risk and even forfeit their own lives to save their brothers in arms. *Greater love hath no man than this...*

Perhaps because of their relative youth, members of the post-9/11 class of Medal of Honor recipients who fought in Afghanistan and Iraq were especially popular with the crowds in Annapolis. Unlike their forebears, they are members of an all-volunteer military that was created after Vietnam with the abolishment of the draft. As socially engineered and self-selected over many years, the force they represent is unlike any that the United States has fielded in the past, let alone during the longest period of extended war in the nation's history.

Many of those troops volunteered after the September 11, 2001, terrorist attacks—the most devastating blow to the homeland since Pearl Harbor—knowing they were signing up for combat. They are mostly the sons and daughters not of Wall Street hedge fund managers or Silicon Valley entrepreneurs, but of working-class cops, teachers, firefighters, and especially other soldiers. One U.S. Army survey found that the 304 general officers in the military had 180 children serving in uniform, making military service something of a family business. By contrast, of the 535 members of Congress at the time of the survey, the country's political elite, fewer than a dozen had children in the services.

The all-volunteer U.S. military hails from all corners of the country, though the South and Mountain West are somewhat disproportionately represented, regions that not coincidentally have venerable traditions of military service and play host to more than their share of major military bases. The ranks of the volunteers are filled disproportionately by African Americans, who account for 17 percent of the active-duty military (versus 13 percent of the U.S. population), largely because military service has long been seen as a step up the socioeconomic ladder in the black community. Hispanics are underrepresented but growing as a proportion of the military ranks at 12 percent (versus 18 percent in the general population). Women are likewise underrepresented (with 15 percent of active-duty ranks) in what remains a male-dominated occupation. Members of the volunteer military are also significantly more fit and better educated than their age cohorts in the civilian population, and less likely to have criminal records.

While they collectively represent less than 1 percent of the population, America's military volunteers have disproportionately shouldered the burden of our nation's longest wars. Not surprisingly, nearly two decades of fighting have made this professional warrior caste, and the military ethos they embrace, stand somewhat distinct from the society they have chosen to defend with their lives. Many have returned home from war the same way they deployed for combat—largely invisible to a distracted nation.

Through the stories of these warriors, readers will become closely acquainted with the volunteers who selflessly answered the call after the 9/11 terrorist attacks, a group that some military historians are already calling "the New Greatest Generation." Their tales chronicle some of the most intense and impactful battles in Afghanistan and Iraq, and trace the sweeping arc of America's longest wars, from initial routs and "Mission Accomplished," to nearly twin defeats against implacable enemies, to hard-fought and largely successful countering "surges" that ultimately ended in a gray zone somewhere between defeat and outright victory. Such are the challenges for a democracy fighting unconventional wars against fanatical global terrorists and allied nationalist insurgents.

This book focuses on the post-9/11 Medal of Honor awardees in part because as a reporter I have covered the wars in Iraq and Afghanistan, and I have found the example set by our brave volunteers ennobling. I have also talked to generals who question whether the nation would ever have invaded Iraq, or still be fighting in Afghanistan after nineteen years, if we still had a draft army to bring the pain and grief of war home to Middle America and to Washington, D.C. But that's a subject for another book. This one began with a phone call from the Department of the Navy offering an exclusive interview with new Medal of Honor recipient and Navy SEAL chief Britt Slabinski, whose gripping and tragic tale of a fight on a mountain called Takur Ghar in the early days of the "global war on terror" inspired me to seek out the stories of more of these extraordinary individuals, whenever possible expressed in their own voices, and in the case of posthumous awards through the voices of their brothers in arms and families.

Some have detailed their experiences in full-length books that are also cited in these pages.

For a generation of Americans who have come of age in the all-volunteer era, war has become an abstraction, something best left to the professionals. In airports and train stations we politely tell those in uniform, "Thank you for your service," knowing full well that their sacrifice and that of their families makes it possible for the vast majority of us not to serve. My hope is that the stories of these remarkable individuals will remind readers that war is never an abstraction, and we owe it to all the men and women who fight on our behalf to acknowledge and honor their sacrifice.

Men like Marine Corps corporal William "Kyle" Carpenter, still the youngest living Medal of Honor recipient. In Afghanistan in 2010, a twenty-one-year-old Carpenter purposely lunged toward a Taliban hand grenade in order to shield his buddy from the blast. He endured more than forty surgeries over three years to recover from the resulting catastrophic injuries.

In Annapolis, Carpenter took time out from the Medal of Honor Society festivities to speak to students at the Severn School. He shared with them the wisdom of a young life that, on a faraway battlefield, he had long ago surrendered to God.

"It took a life-changing event to get me to truly appreciate the precious and amazing life I have been blessed with," Carpenter told the students. "Please take it from me, enjoy every day to the fullest, don't take life too seriously, always try and make it count, appreciate the small and simple things, be kind and help others, let the ones you love know you love them, and when things get hard trust there is a bigger plan and that you will be stronger for it."

After his speech at the Severn School, Kyle Carpenter shook hands and spoke at length with Kevin Looney, whose son, Navy lieutenant Brendan Looney, was killed in Afghanistan. Kyle knew he represented a living connection to a place and a cause that was forever etched in a grieving father's heart. Later, as the crowd around him grew, Carpenter saw an old friend walk into the gymnasium. He went over and hugged Zachary Stinson, his former squad leader in Afghanistan, who lost both legs above the knee from the blast of an improvised explosive device. He and Carpenter had leaned on each other for support during the excruciating years of recovery.

When the crowd finally dispersed, Carpenter turned to a reporter who was present. "I'm so honored and appreciative of the Medal of Honor," he said. "It's not mine. It truly represents Zach, everyone who served in uniform who died and bled for our country. It's such an incredibly heavy medal to wear."

IN THE COMPANY OF HEROES

Greater love hath no man than this, that a man lay down his life for his friends.

JOHN 15:13 (KJV)

Chapter 1

———☆———

Where Angels Fear to Tread

Navy Senior Chief (SEAL) Britt K. Slabinski

Air Force Technical Sergeant
John A. Chapman

Sometimes at night they huddled over a portable chess set in the dusty tent they shared, their cots pulled close together, heads bent over a board game that offered blessed respite from the ceaseless hours of preparation and worry. They plotted their next chess moves, talked about their children and families back home, and, for a few stolen minutes, tuned out the near-constant roar of helicopters launching nearby, the acrid smell of burning jet fuel and the crush of stacked combat gear—the rumblings of a gun outfit on the eve of a big fight.

Though they hailed from different Special Forces branches, Navy SEAL team leader Britt Slabinski and Air Force Combat Controller John Chapman would have been indistinguishable to the casual observer. Both young men sported beards and nondescript camouflage uniforms with few markings, and they carried themselves with athletic swagger, all signatures of special operations forces. As they sparred good-naturedly over the chess set in February 2002, the idea that these two friends would each receive the nation's highest award for valor for their actions in the coming days would have seemed preposterous.

Despite choosing different services, Slabinski and Chapman followed similar paths from all-American boyhood to a secret base camp in the foothills of the Hindu Kush. In fact, they grew up less than fifty miles from each other.

Slabinski was a second-generation SEAL (Sea, Air, and

Land) commando whose father had served as an underwater demolition expert. Growing up in Northampton, Massachusetts, the young Slabinski became an Eagle Scout at the tender age of fourteen, achieving the highest rank in the Boy Scouts and developing an early thirst for adventure. A possible outlet was suggested during junior high school, when he joined his father for a reunion of his SEAL Team in Little Neck, Virginia. Watching his father reconnect instantly with his former brothers in arms, sensing their timeless bonds of camaraderie, the young Slabinski yearned for that sense of belonging and devotion to a greater cause. When his friends went off to college or started day jobs after high school, he found himself drawn instead to the challenge of trying to become an elite Navy SEAL.

The SEALs are direct descendants of the Navy's Operational Swimmers, Raiders, and Underwater Demolition Teams who distinguished themselves during World War II. Those unconventional warriors were forged out of necessity and the hard lessons of tragedy. During the Marine Corps' landing on Tarawa atoll in the South Pacific in 1943, an armada of landing craft was unexpectedly stuck on a reef and left exposed by a low tide. Forced to try to wade ashore, many Marines drowned or were slaughtered by heavy Japanese fire before ever reaching the beach. Due to errant Allied bombardment of German beach defenses in Normandy, more than half of the men in the Naval Combat Demolition Unit that landed on Omaha Beach on D-Day were killed or wounded. The missions and tactics of today's SEALs were developed in part as a reaction to those experiences. They include advanced beach reconnaissance, fire support "overwatch," and explosive destruction of underwater obstacles for amphibious landings.

From that heritage, the U.S. Navy SEALs were officially christened in 1962 by President John F. Kennedy, who is considered the spiritual father of U.S. special operations forces. At the height of the Cold War between allied democracies and communist dictatorships—and with a war in Vietnam looming on the horizon—Kennedy foresaw the need for unconventional forces steeped in the tactics of guerrilla warfare. His administration thus greatly expanded the Army Special Forces "Green Berets," and created two SEAL Teams out of existing Navy Underwater Demolition Teams. Both the Green Berets and the Navy SEALs largely came into their own during direct action missions and fierce fighting in Vietnam. The North Vietnamese and Viet Cong dubbed the stealthy SEALs "the men with the green faces" because of their camouflage face paint and warrior spirit.

As a raw enlistee, Britt Slabinski stood on a beach with roughly one hundred other young men at the Naval Special Warfare Center in Coronado, California, each of them determined to join that storied force of unconventional warriors. All of them believed they had the grit and determination to complete BUD/S (Basic Underwater Demolition/SEAL) training, the notoriously difficult gateway to becoming a Navy SEAL. Yet after completing eight weeks of basic conditioning, more than half of the trainees "rang the bell" during "Hell Week," unable to cope with a grueling crucible of sleep deprivation, exhaustion, and physical pain that purposely pushes trainees beyond their limits and into uncharted realms of misery.

As he proudly stood in his dress Navy uniform on BUD/S class graduation day, Britt Slabinski had looked around to see only roughly twenty of his original training class still standing. From that moment on, being a Navy SEAL just felt like home.

Britt Slabinski never looked back.

John Chapman was a small-town kid from Windsor Locks, Connecticut, a burg of twelve thousand citizens on the banks of the Connecticut River. Early on Chapman showed the athleticism and nerve that earned him All State in diving three out of his four years in high school and made him a standout on the soccer team. To his family and tight-knit circle of friends he was just a happy-go-lucky athlete with an easy smile and winning manner.

After a short stint at the University of Connecticut, Chapman felt himself yearning for more adventure in his life. He didn't find enough of it enlisting in the Air Force and working in front of computers as part of an information systems squadron, so he volunteered for the elite Combat Control Team (CCT) career field. He began the grueling, yearlong Combat Controller training program at Lackland Air Force Base, Texas. From then on, he didn't complain about a lack of adventure in his life.

Like the Naval Special Warfare units, the Air Force's Combat Control Teams grew out of bitter lessons from World War II, most specifically a disastrous airborne assault in 1943 on the island of Sicily. Roughly seven hundred paratroopers were mistakenly dropped out at sea over the Mediterranean, where many of them drowned. Numerous aircraft involved in the operation nearly flew into each other on their approaches. Given the obvious need for more accurate airdrops, the U.S. Army created the Pathfinders, reconnaissance scouts who secretly infiltrated to an objective before the main assault forces arrived. Once in place, they provided visual guidance to inbound aircraft and jumpers with flares, high-powered lights, and smoke pots. When the Air Force became a separate service in 1947, the Pathfinders went with the air arm to provide the nascent service with expertise in air traffic control and airborne operations. The Pathfinders were later renamed Combat Control Teams.

Even a gifted athlete like John Chapman found CCT training daunting. There was the highly technical Combat Control Operator Course in air traffic control, air navigation, and communication procedures. That was followed by a rigorous, weeks-long course at the Air Force Survival School at Fairchild Air Force Base, Washington, where Chapman and his classmates received instruction on how to survive on their own in harsh climates and conditions. At the Army's Airborne School at Fort Benning, Georgia, Chapman learned basic parachuting skills necessary for infiltration behind enemy lines. Combat Control School instructors at Pope Air Force Base,

North Carolina, taught Chapman and his teammates small unit tactics, fire support, demolition, and land navigation.

After initial training, Chapman graduated to Special Tactics Advanced Skills Training, which includes training in free-fall parachuting at the Military Free-Fall Parachutist Course School at Fort Bragg, North Carolina. He also completed the Air Force Combat Dive Course, and he taught at the Naval Diving and Salvage Training Center in Panama City, Florida. On top of mastering skills such as establishing aircraft landing zones and parachute drop zones, and calling in ordnance from ground-attack aircraft, Chapman ultimately became a military free-fall parachutist, a static line jumpmaster, and a military scuba dive supervisor.

At one point when John Chapman's rapidly dwindling class of would-be Combat Controllers was undergoing particularly tough scuba diving drills, someone asked their chief CCT instructor, Master Sergeant Ron Childress, whether he was actually trying to train them to become Navy SEALs.

"No," Childress replied. "I'm training you so you don't slow the SEALs down."

The dropout rate for Combat Controller training was similar to that of the SEALs, and when Chapman received the signature red beret of Air Force Combat Controllers, only six other members of his class remained. Yet his instructors never doubted that Chapman would earn the Combat Control Badge and embody its motto: "First There." John Chapman was quiet and unassuming, but he had the cocky attitude and swagger common to all good Combat Controllers. By the end of training, he and his remaining teammates had transformed into airpower-savvy commandos who could run, jump, or swim with members of any other special operations unit, and act as their conduit for close air support and insertion and extraction by air.

For the Special Forces community, one of the most intriguing quirks of the job was watching cable news reports on hot spots around the world and having a pretty good idea where they would soon deploy. Special Forces operators even used secret code words with their wives that alerted them to turn on the television to see where their husbands were likely going next.

On the morning of September 11, 2001, no one needed a code word to know to turn on their television. Navy senior chief petty officer Britt Slabinski was working out at a gym in Virginia Beach with his SEAL teammates when someone directed their attention to a nearby screen. Commercial airliners were flying into the World Trade Center towers and the Pentagon out of a clear blue sky. Technical Sergeant John Chapman was watching the same horror show at Pope Air Force Base, where he was stationed. Both men understood that the swift sword of U.S. retribution would soon cast its shadow over a landlocked country of towering mountains and verdant river valleys on the other side of the world. Before they had even received the official deployment orders, they began packing their gear for Afghanistan.

✯ ✯ ✯

In late February 2002 the Special Forces camp at Gardiz was a frenetic hub of activity. Up until that time America's self-proclaimed global war on terror had mostly been a rout. A relative handful of U.S. Special Forces troops, backed by over-whelming U.S. airpower and allied with local Afghan militias, had toppled the Taliban regime in a matter of weeks. They'd had Osama bin Laden and his top Al Qaeda lieutenants sur-rounded and all but captured or killed a few months earlier at Tora Bora, before allowing them to slip away. Everyone antici-pated more of the same in the battle that was then brewing.

For more than a month, U.S. signals and human intelli-gence had indicated a large concentration of Al Qaeda and Taliban fighters in a steep, mountainous valley along the Afghan-Pakistan border called the Shah-i-Kot, or "Place of the King." There were also indications that high-value Al Qaeda leaders and allied Taliban warlords were wintering in the val-ley, possibly in preparation for a spring offensive once the snows melted and the fighting season began in earnest.

The U.S. response was Operation Anaconda. From the beginning, the battle plan was designed to rectify the mis-takes of the battle for Tora Bora, when U.S. commanders had counted on unreliable Afghan militias to close the noose on Osama bin Laden. The intent of the aptly named operation was to essentially encircle the enemy first before squeezing the life out of them.

Anaconda was the first set-piece battle of the post-9/11 era involving both U.S. Special Forces and conventional units. Ele-ments of the U.S. 10th Mountain Division and allied Afghan militias planned to launch a surprise push down the valley from one direction, while elements of the 101st Airborne Division would intercept fleeing enemy fighters from blocking positions in the other direction. The name given to the two task forces revealed their intended effect—"Hammer" and "Anvil." As they had at Tora Bora, the 150 to 200 Al Qaeda and Taliban fighters estimated to occupy villages in the valley were expected to flee U.S. forces wielding overwhelming firepower. Only this time they would have nowhere to escape.

U.S. commanders did not know at the time that as many as a thousand Al Qaeda and Taliban fighters were actually waiting for them in the Shah-i-Kot. During the Soviet-Afghan War in the 1980s, mujahedeen fighters and foreign jihadists had built interconnected trench and bunker systems on the rocky hillsides overlooking the valley floor, fortifications that allowed them to defeat superior Red Army forces not once, but twice. Those mujahedeen and foreign jihadists were the forebears of the Taliban and Al Qaeda, whose seasoned fighters at that moment were taking up carefully calibrated firing positions in the familiar bunkers, trenches, and ridgelines of the Shah-i-Kot.

They had no intention of fleeing.

As preparation for Operation Anaconda, small reconnaissance, or "recce," teams of Navy SEALs and Army Special Forces were inserted at strategic locations in the mountains of the Shah-i-Kot. Their mission was to report on the movement of enemy forces and direct airstrikes on Al Qaeda and Taliban positions. Despite their efforts the initial push by U.S. conventional and Afghan militia forces into the valley in early March was met with unexpectedly stiff resistance, and it stalled under withering machine-gun and mortar fire from the hillsides. U.S. commanders called for the urgent insertion of more recce teams.

In the early morning of March 4, it was the turn of "Mako 30," the SEAL team led by Britt Slabinski that included John Chapman. As they changed into their "battle rattle" and grabbed their weapons to take to the launch pad, Slabinski noted the pieces still arrayed on their chessboard. With all the activity, he and Chapman had never managed to finish the game.

The twin rotors of the MH-47E Chinook helicopter labored in the thin air as it ascended to the top of a prominent eleven-thousand-foot mountain called Takur Gar. The peak offered unobstructed views of the southern approaches of the Shah-i-Kot, and a clear line of sight to the village of Marzak a few kilometers away. Team leader Slabinski's plan was to set down at a safe distance from the peak and climb stealthily the rest of the way to the top of the mountain, making a "controlled approach" and using the darkness as cover.

Yet no battle plan ever completely survives the firing of the first shot. Maintenance problems with one of the helicopters involved in the operation and a nearby B-52 bombing strike delayed the insertion of the commandos and compressed already tight timelines. In order to position and conceal themselves before daybreak, Mako 30 would have to be inserted by air directly onto the mountaintop. Earlier surveillance from a Predator drone indicated that the area was clear, but Slabinski knew that the risk factor of the mission had climbed significantly. He recognized the knifelike ridge at the peak of Takur Gar as a nearly perfect spot to observe the Anaconda battlespace. Someone else might have recognized it too.

It was nearly 3 a.m. when the Chinook helicopter carrying Mako 30, code-named "Razor 3," began to touch down over the snow-covered landing zone. Slabinski and his team untethered themselves from safe lines as a mixture of frigid air and engine backwash poured through the open rear door. Then they lurched as a deafening explosion suddenly rocked the aircraft. The inside quickly filled with dense smoke. Razor 3 had taken a direct hit from a rocket-propelled grenade (RPG). The staccato thud of machine-gun rounds raked the fuselage like hammer blows.

The aircraft swung crazily as the pilots fought to regain control, fluid spewing from severed hydraulic and fuel lines. In the smoke Slabinski saw Petty Officer First Class Neil Roberts slip before being grabbed by a crew chief who was still tethered to his safe line. A sudden burst of power from the pilots as they tried to escape the ambush sent Roberts and the crew chief sliding off the back ramp. Crew members scrambled to pull their colleague back inside the helicopter by his tether, but he could not keep his grip on the Navy SEAL. Neil Roberts had fallen into a hot landing zone crawling with enemy fighters.

The "Night Stalker" pilots from the 160th Special Operations Aviation Regiment veered sharply away from the landing zone, still struggling to get the aircraft back under control. They scanned the terrain through night-vision goggles and searched for someplace among the jagged rocks to bring the crippled helicopter down. Roughly five miles away they saw a relatively flat patch of mountainside and prepared to execute a controlled crash landing.

Britt Slabinski was looking out the window, bracing himself instinctively as the ground seemed to leap crazily up to meet them. The next thing he remembered was getting off the floor of the helicopter and directing his team to secure the crash site. He took a head count to confirm what they all knew—Neil Roberts was missing. On top of his original mission to supply overwatch for the Battle of Anaconda, Slabinski now had a missing teammate and a downed aircrew to worry about. Tech Sergeant John Chapman was on his radio directing an AC-130 gunship to provide air cover of the crash site, and he arranged for another helicopter to collect them. When they were airborne once again, Slabinski realized that he would soon have to make a decision that would test the judgment of Solomon.

Back at the Special Forces camp at Gardiz, Slabinski sat on the rear ramp of the MH-47 Chinook helicopter in the dark. Propellers whirled overhead. He could feel the rivets digging into his backside as he tried to clear his mind. So far that night, Mako 30 had been ambushed by Al Qaeda fighters, lost a man on a barren mountaintop in the Hindu Kush, and survived a controlled helicopter crash in enemy territory. And it was still more than an hour before dawn.

The lives of his men and the fate of a mission that had gone awry nearly from the start hung on Chief Petty Officer Britt Slabinski's next decision. He studied his notebook and tried to bring order to a tactical situation that was stacked against his team and promised tragedy from every angle. Surveillance from an AC-130 gunship flying over Takur Gar indicated that his teammate Neil Roberts was still alive and surrounded by nearby enemy fighters. Everyone understood Roberts's fate if he was captured by Al Qaeda. Slabinski had also learned the hard way that the Al Qaeda force dug in atop Takur Gar had his small team badly outnumbered and outgunned.

At that altitude, the battlespace was frigid and blanketed in snow. To reach Roberts, they would almost certainly have to fight uphill through snowdrifts. Slabinski could wait until the quick reaction force of Army Rangers arrived to help even the odds, but he doubted that Neil Roberts had that much time. On the other hand, Slabinski was responsible for all of the commandos in his SEAL team as well as for the Army pilots who would have to fly them back to the top of a mountain where ambushers awaited.

Slabinski looked at his notepad and tried to sort through this Gordian knot of responsibilities when a thought intruded into his careful calculations and refused to leave. It was the old pledge he learned by heart as an Eagle Scout: *On my honor I will do my best to do my duty…On my honor I will do my best…On my honor…*

The Boy Scout pledge kept reeling through Slabinski's thoughts unbidden, until he suddenly sat up straight and started to listen to the voice in his head. At that moment he decided to go get Neil Roberts—or, probably, to die trying. He simply hadn't yet done his best to try and rescue his teammate. As if coming out of a trance, he realized that the helicopter was still running and burning fuel, and they had perhaps forty-five minutes before it would need to be refueled. They had to act fast.

John Chapman and the other four SEALs were sitting inside the darkened MH-47 Chinook when Slabinski strode up the rear ramp and told the crew chief to turn the lights on inside the aircraft. The members of Mako 30 gathered around their leader.

"Eyes on me!" Slabinski shouted over the din of the rotors. "Eyes on me!"

There was no time to debate the decision. Slabinski made sure he had the entire team's attention, and then he laid out the daunting tactical situation and told them of his decision to return to Takur Gar to try and rescue Neil Roberts. As he looked straight into the faces of John Chapman and each of the other SEAL commandos, they all nodded their heads in the affirmative. Not one member of the team hesitated or flinched from the decision, despite heavy odds that it amounted to a death sentence.

"Okay, let's go do this," one of the SEALs said, summarizing the reactions of the team.

On the flight back up Takur Gar, Britt Slabinski sat in the rear of the Razor 4 Chinook. He grabbed a piston attached to the back ramp and leaned out into the cold night, looking at the imposing mountain in the near distance, its snow-covered peak luminous through the prism of night-vision goggles. *This is such a majestic fucking mountain*, he thought to himself. *Isn't it ironic the ugliness that is about to be unleashed on its pinnacle?*

With the steep mountainsides unspooling outside the rear door in a dizzying kaleidoscope, Slabinski's thoughts finally started to slow down. He felt with absolute certainty that this was a one-way trip up Takur Gar, not only for himself but likely for his teammates too. But they were the only chance that Neil Roberts had, slim as it was. They had to play it out. Slabinski thought of his six-year-old son, Bryce, back home, and of his family. He could see clearly in his mind's eye the Navy chaplain and men in blue knocking on his front door, and the stricken faces of his family.

Slabinski's thoughts turned to his son. *I love you, Bryce, be great*, he thought. *And I'm sorry for what's about to come.*

And then Britt Slabinski parked it in a corner of his mind and shut the door, and for the rest of the trip the Navy SEAL team leader stared out the back of the helicopter and mentally prepared for the task at hand.

★ ★ ★

Razor 4 settled over the hot landing zone in the darkness and immediately machine-gun fire punctured the fuselage. As he was taking off his headset, Slabinski heard the Night Stalker pilot "Al"—the same pilot who had been shot out of the sky earlier over Takur Gar, and insisted on returning—shout into the intercom.

"Team leader, good luck!"

Slabinski was the first off the back ramp. He jumped down into fresh snow past his knees and tried to run. A few heavy steps and he tumbled into a drift, his night-vision goggles smashing into his face and splitting his nose open. As he got up and tried to clear his goggles of snow and blood, he thought this was some unlucky way to start.

John Chapman was the next man out of the helicopter. As the Al Qaeda machine gunners focused their fire on the departing helicopter, Chapman charged up the hillside toward the nearest fortified bunker under a tree, firing his M4 automatic rifle as he went. Slabinski was close behind trying to provide him cover. Without hesitation Chapman darted into the bunker and shot two surprised Al Qaeda fighters at point-blank range. His quick reaction almost certainly saved the entire team from being cut to pieces by the machine gun before reaching cover.

"John, what do you got?" Slabinski shouted when he reached the bunker.

"I don't know!" Chapman replied, his head on a swivel.

A tongue of flame licked out of the dark maw of a bunker hidden beneath another tree just ten meters away. The force of the impact knocked Chapman to the ground. Slabinski felt the bullets passing through his clothing and gear, smashing his medical kit and rattling his body armor. Taking cover behind a large rock outcrop, he peered around and saw John Chapman's motionless body.

Scanning the scene to gather situational awareness, Slabinski saw enemy muzzle flashes to his front, left, and right, where his teammates were engaging other bunkers. They were essentially in a fishbowl, with entrenched enemy machine gunners firing down on them from three sides. The air crackled with whistling projectiles, the impacts cracking off rock and kicking up snow geysers in every direction.

Slabinski knew he had to silence the machine-gun bunker directly to his front or they would have little chance of making it off the mountainside. He grabbed a grenade from his pocket and darted from behind the rock to toss it at the bunker. The echo of the explosion was still reverberating when the machine gun recommenced firing. On the second attempt, Slabinski risked a few extra steps of exposure before arcing the grenade directly over the tarp covering the bunker. He saw it roll down the tarp. After the explosion the machine gun fell mercifully silent. Relieved, Slabinski grabbed his rifle and had trained it on the bunker when he saw the muzzle flash of the machine gun again and dove back behind the rock. *Dammit!*

Out of hand grenades, Slabinski grabbed his 40mm grenade launcher. The range was too close to target the nearest bunker, so he aimed the snub-nosed weapon at the enemy muzzle flashes in the near distance to suppress some of the fire pinning down his teammates. After exhausting his six 40mm grenades he threw the launcher in the snow.

The suppressive fire allowed the SEAL team's M60 machine gunner, "Brett," to reach the rock outcrop. There were tactics for taking out a gun emplacement. Slabinski told Brett to pour enfilading fire from right to left into the bunker to provide cover. Slabinski and another SEAL commando would flank it from the left side. At the given signal Brett exposed himself atop the rock and fired directly into the bunker from nearly point-blank range, the red-hot brass of the 7.62mm shell casings peppering Slabinski in the face as he rolled away. Before he could flank the bunker there was an explosion from an enemy grenade. When the snow and smoke cleared, Brett was nowhere to be seen. He shouted out from behind the rock that he was wounded.

After he repositioned himself behind the rock once again, Slabinski heard his SEAL teammate "Kyle" shout out:

"Hey, Slab, I just had the eyelet of my boot shot off!"

Slabinski took stock of their situation. John Chapman's body lay motionless nearby where he had been cut down by the machine gun. Brett was wounded and bleeding from multiple grenade fragments. There was no sign of Neil Roberts. And they were still caught in the crossfire of several bunkers.

With bullets whistling all around, a feeling came over Britt

Slabinski that his guys on this mountaintop were getting deci-mated. He had to do something to change the situation or they were going to die. He decided to relocate the team to the rear over a small lip and depression in the mountainside that might offer better cover. He used the radio to call in suppressing fire from an AC-130 gunship circling overhead. The aircraft's can-nons and 25mm Gatling gun opened up with tracers raining fire on the mountaintop, and he shouted for his guys to start moving. Before leaving the cover of the rock, he crawled right on top of John Chapman's body, looking for some movement or any sign of life. He got nothing. John was gone.

As the remaining team trudged through the snow toward the indentation some twenty yards down the mountain, the Al Qaeda machine gun erupted again. Impact geysers tracked them until one of the SEALs was cut down with a direct hit that nearly ripped off his leg. Slabinski and another SEAL grabbed their wounded teammate by his body armor and dragged him over the lip, his blood staining the snow and leaving a trail of gore.

In the small indentation the SEAL team was out of the machine gunner's line of sight, but they were still taking frag-mentation fire from an unknown source. Slabinski radioed the AC-130 gunship, suspecting that they might have lost the team's position and were getting too close with friendly fire.

"No, we still have your position," came the reply from the AC-130. "But there's now an enemy mortar we can see that is targeting you."

Beyond exhaustion and with a rage tinged with grief, Britt

Slabinski longed to shout to the heavens, *Well, what else do you have in store for me?* Instead, the SEAL team leader relocated his team farther down the mountain where there was an outcropping of rocks that provided better cover, and then helped tend to the wounded. Brett the M-60 machine gunner was wounded in both legs by grenade fragments. They applied a field tourniquet to the SEAL hit by the machine gun, who would surely lose his leg. Because there was no place safe enough to bring in a medivac helicopter, they would have to try and carry or drag the man down the snow-covered mountain.

The sun was starting to crest the ridgeline of Takur Gar, and Slabinski tried to raise the quick reaction force (QRF) on the radio, knowing that they were under way and would soon arrive on scene. Unbeknownst to the SEAL team, a series of communications failures, owing both to faulty equipment and disconnects between various headquarters, kept the QRF helicopters from receiving the message that Mako 30 had repositioned down the mountain. The QRF believed that the SEAL commandos were still engaged on top of Takur Gar, where two helicopters had already been shot to pieces.

As he was barking into the radio, Slabinski saw the first QRF Chinook round the mountainside and bank directly over their heads. The dark green behemoth flew by so close that he could count the rivets in the fuselage like a dragon's scales. *That's not good*, he thought with alarm, *they are headed right into the ambush zone.* He frantically tried to switch from the AC-130's close air support radio frequency to the different frequency used by the QRF helicopter pilots, hoping to wave them off.

Before Slabinski could connect with the lead helicopter, an explosion reverberated on the mountaintop. One of the SEAL teammates who still had eyes on the landing zone some fifty yards up the slope confirmed Slabinski's worst fears.

"The QRF just took an RPG!" he shouted. "They're down!"

As the sound of intense gunfire erupted on the top of Takur Gar, Slabinski was able to reach the second QRF helicopter by radio and wave it off. He directed them to a finger of flat ground just below the SEALs' position, and the helicopter landed and disembarked the Ranger platoon that would eventually secure the mountain.

SEAL team leader Britt Slabinski's decision to return to Takur Gar to rescue Neil Roberts heroically embodied the U.S. military's ethos of "leave no man behind," and he valiantly led his battered men off the mountain. And yet improbably and contrary to everything he thought he knew, his team's fight did not end there. Compelling evidence from an improbable witness would later suggest that a member of Mako 30 still fought on at the top of Takur Gar.

High above the frigid mountain peak a wasplike drone circled unseen. There were only a handful of MQ-1 Predators in the U.S. arsenal at the time, and they represented the leading edge of a revolution in air reconnaissance and surveillance. Able to loiter over a target for more than twenty hours, the Predator used its infrared video camera as an unblinking eye in the sky, bouncing its signal off a satellite to ground stations that rerouted its video feed around the world in seconds via fiber optic cables. The imagery broadcast by the Predator circling Takur Gar on March 4, and the narrative it supported, would ultimately lead to the first U.S. airman receiving the Medal of Honor since the Vietnam War.

John Chapman's body lay as still as death for twelve minutes. No one approached the bunker where he lay, and yet the Predator video suddenly captured movement there. Around that time another Air Force Combat Controller attached to a nearby Delta Force reconnaissance team began to hear faint distress calls on his satellite radio, repeated over and over. "This is Mako Three Zero Charlie...This is Mako Three Zero Charlie...This is Mako Three Zero Charlie." In a later sworn affidavit to Air Force investigators, the Combat Controller "Jay" confirmed that he immediately recognized both the call sign and the voice. It was definitely Tech Sergeant John Chapman.

"I distinctly heard Mako 30 transmitting," Jay, who had served in the same unit as Chapman for years, told investigators. "This occurred over a 40-minute period. I am absolutely positive that [it] was John's voice. I have no doubt whatsoever."

In the Predator's grainy black-and-white video, the figure presumed to be Chapman moves about the bunker firing at multiple targets. A low-light video camera in the AC-130 gunship circling overhead also picked up the signature "glint tape" and body "strobe" designed to identify a U.S. commando on the ground, and it registered the laser rangefinder of a U.S.-issued M4 rifle firing from the bunker. Air Force targeting analysis would count thirty-nine distinct muzzle flashes from Chapman's M4 automatic during this time. The Delta Force reconnaissance team also intercepted radio traffic from the Al Qaeda fighters talking about an "American" still on the mountaintop, and how to eliminate him. Twice, Al Qaeda fighters appeared to sneak up on the bunker, before being killed at point-blank range.

By the time Razor 1 carrying the quick reaction force appeared on the scene, Chapman had been wounded multiple times and was nearly out of ammunition. The sun had started to crest the peak of Takur Gar, leaving the Chinook helicopter exposed and at the mercy of entrenched Al Qaeda gunners. Seemingly with no thought for his own life, Chapman left the safety of his bunker in order to engage two Al Qaeda fighters on the ridgeline armed with rocket-propelled grenades, exposing himself to the machine gunner only yards away. The Chinook was hit by an RPG but was able to put down in a controlled crash. Chapman was cut down with two fatal rounds in his back.

On recovery, John Chapman's body was surrounded by empty 30-round magazines. He had all but exhausted his 210 rounds of ammunition. An autopsy would later reveal that he was shot nine times, seven of the wounds definitely suffered while he was still alive. Chapman also had a broken nose and abrasions that suggested hand-to-hand combat.

★ ★ ★

The duty to deliver the knock on the door that every service member's family dreads fell to Lieutenant Colonel Kenneth Rodriguez, commander of the Air Force's 24th Special Tactics Squadron. When Chapman's wife, Valerie, opened the door with her young daughters, Madison and Brianna, Rodriguez had to tell them that John would not be coming home from war. Many years later the searing memory still brought him to tears. "When I saw those beautiful little girls that were just five and three [years old] at the time, I thought, 'You know they are going to grow up without their daddy,'" Rodriguez recalled. "I think of that every time I think of John."

John Chapman's father, Gene, later sent Rodriguez and the rest of his squadron of Combat Controllers a letter. "We may look at what John did and say he is a hero, but then we are not one of his team or the other teams that go in where angels wouldn't tread," the elder Chapman wrote. "John is proud to be part of you, and if you could ask him right now, he would tell you what he did was for his family, friends, and the teams he worked with. Most of all he did what he did for his country."

In many ways, what became known as the Battle of Roberts Ridge was an inflection point. The sacrifices there foreshadowed the difficult years ahead as the U.S. military confronted a determined global terrorist insurgency, in what would evolve into the longest wars in our nation's history. The lessons learned during the fighting on Roberts Ridge also informs U.S. Special Forces tactics, training, and planning to this day. Above all, the heroism of U.S. forces that day sent an unmistakable message to the Al Qaeda terrorists responsible for the deadliest attack on the U.S. homeland since Pearl Harbor that there was no place they could hide, not even on a remote mountain peak in the Hindu Kush.

The tragedy and confusion of what exactly happened on Roberts Ridge, and who was most deserving of recognition for their actions there, also sparked tension and controversy for years among the service branches within the Special Forces community. The Navy SEALs were understandably reluctant to accept that Chapman might have been mistakenly abandoned on the mountaintop. Many members of the Air Force Special Forces community believed that in the deadly chaos, it may actually have been Neil Roberts's dead body that Slabinski crawled over in the dark.

After more than sixteen years, those tensions were finally laid to rest. Following an exhaustive review of all the available evidence, Defense Secretary James Mattis concluded that both Navy SEAL Britt Slabinski and Air Force Combat Controller John Chapman were deserving of the nation's highest award for valor. Slabinski and Chapman's family received their Medals of Honor at White House ceremonies in the spring and summer of 2018.

On first learning the news of the award, Chapman's wife, Valerie Nessel, said that if John were still alive, he would want to recognize the other men who lost their lives that day. "Even though he did something he will be awarded the Medal of Honor for he would not want those other guys to be forgotten.

They were part of a team together. And I think he would say that the Medal of Honor is not just for him, but for all the guys who were lost on that mountain."

For the record, seven elite U.S. Special Forces troops were killed in action during the intense, fifteen-hour firefight on Roberts Ridge. The fallen include the battle's namesake, Navy SEAL Neil Roberts, who was executed soon after being captured by Al Qaeda fighters; Army Rangers in the quick reaction force Sergeant Bradley Crose, Corporal Matthew Commons, and Specialist Marc Anderson; Sergeant Philip Svitak of the Army's 160th Special Operations Aviation Regiment; Air Force pararescueman Jason Cunningham; and Air Force Combat Controller John Chapman.

In an interview with the author, Britt Slabinski said his Medal of Honor reflects on the valor of all the U.S. Special Forces operators who fought on Takur Gar that day, the living and the dead. "All my guys followed me up the mountain that day, as did the aircrews that kept the flights coming, and the Rangers who came not because they knew us, but because they knew we were in trouble," he said. "In many ways I'm uncomfortable being singled out because when you wrap your head around that whole battle, every one of them deserved this medal. That's no exaggeration."

When asked for his reaction to evidence suggesting that John Chapman survived his initial wounds that terrible morning and fought on in a manner that would unite the two former tentmates and chess partners in the world's most exclusive ring of valor, Slabinski was pensive.

"Not a day goes by when I don't think about John," he said. "There was no doubt in my mind that he was dead. No doubt in my mind. But my first thought [on hearing of that possibility] was that it would be completely in John's character to have done that. That was his DNA. That was my whole team's DNA. It's not what I saw. Not what I experienced. But it was within John Chapman's character to have done those things."

Chapter 2

——✫——

The Gates of Baghdad

Army Sergeant First Class Paul R. Smith

The moon was only a sliver in the early morning dark of April 2, 2003, as the armored spearhead of the U.S. invasion of Iraq tried to thread a division-sized force through the eye of a needle called the Karbala Gap. The 3rd Infantry Division had already traveled farther in less time than any division-sized force in the history of modern warfare, its scores of M1 tanks, Bradley Fighting Vehicles, and M113 armored personnel carriers churning over three hundred kilometers in a matter of days before pausing to resupply for this final assault on the Iraqi capital of Baghdad. From the very beginning, battle planners had identified the most perilous potential chokepoint in the entire operation as the Karbala Gap.

On the night of April 2, the tight confines of the gap between the city of Karbala and a vast lake to the west called the Bahr al-Milh amplified the percussive sounds of nearby battle and the clanking of armor as hundreds of tanks and personnel carriers trundled over the broken terrain. To the east, an armored task force was screening the town of Karbala and repelling a slew of determined Iraqi assault teams. The rest of the lead 1st Brigade felt its way across the pitted and uneven terrain to two earthen dams. Everyone was tensed for the batten-down alert signaling that incoming Iraqi artillery carried chemical weapons or nerve gas, because if ever Saddam Hussein decided to unleash those weapons for maximum effect the confines of the gap offered his best opportunity.

There was even intelligence that the Iraqis might blow the dam that bordered the gap from the west, sending the black waters of the Bahr al-Milh cascading down to sweep away the invaders.

Despite sporadic Iraqi rocket and artillery fire, lead elements of the 3rd Infantry made it through the Karbala Gap, meeting only light resistance. Planners had anticipated that passage through the gap might require as much as twenty-four hours of fighting, but it had been accomplished in less than five. The next day U.S. commanders discovered that elements of the Republican Guard Medina Division had decided instead to contest the U.S. advance at a strategic bridge crossing over the Euphrates River on the other side of the gap labeled Objective Peach.

Iraqi forces successfully blew a hole in the bridge with rigged explosives and kept U.S. troops at bay with tank and mortar fire while attempting to finish the demolition job. Desperate to save the bridge and maintain the furious pace of the offensive, 1st Brigade commanders gave an order not heard from U.S. Army officers since World War II: They called for an assault-boat crossing of a river under heavy enemy fire.

In the ensuing battle, the 3rd Infantry Division's combat engineers added a new chapter to the storied legends of their trade. With artillery-borne smoke charges providing cover, the combat engineers launched their boats into the enveloping fog over the Euphrates. Forty-five minutes of intense fighting erupted that included virtually every form of fire detailed in the Army's warfighting manual, from direct to indirect fire and virtually everything in between—rockets, tank rounds, mortars, missiles, artillery, small-arms, and machine-gun fire.

In the midst of the battle the Euphrates bridge seemed to float just above the fog, hanging tenuously in the balance. Beneath the mists, U.S. combat engineers in rafts or standing in water up to their shoulders frantically cut wires and disabled the Iraqi demolition charges. Finally, the order was given for the brigade's M1 tanks and Bradley Fighting Vehicles to cross the damaged bridge and secure the far side. By sunset on April 3, the last seriously contested gate on the road to Baghdad was flung wide open, paving the way for the long-planned assault on the queen of the chessboard for Operation Iraqi Freedom: "Objective Lions," also known as Saddam International Airport.

After being called back from leave in January 2003 to prepare his troops for Operation Iraqi Freedom, Army sergeant first class Paul Ray Smith relentlessly drilled the men of B Company, 11th Engineer Battalion. The U.S. Army had long before adopted the ethos of the Roman legions, whose "drills were bloodless battles, and their battles bloody drills." The Army's noncommissioned officers were the primary stewards of that code. Smith pushed his men to near exhaustion in training, repeating drills over and over again to make sure his platoon was proficient on the firing range and prepared for the urban combat likely to come. As one of his soldiers put it, "Sergeant

Smith was hard in training because he knew we had to be hard in battle."

As one of the most experienced noncoms in the battalion, Smith was looked up to by younger soldiers anxious about their first combat. He had enlisted in the Army in 1989 and fought in the 1991 Persian Gulf War before logging hardship deployments in Bosnia and Kosovo. He could be a tough taskmaster—that came with the job description—but when a soldier felt the world crashing down on their shoulders, as soldiers sometimes do, Paul Ray Smith would sit them down and find a way to help.

One Christmas, the wife of one of Smith's soldiers had unanticipated surgery, and the parents were unable to provide presents and a traditional holiday meal for their children. Sergeant Smith collected food from the company Christmas party, and he and his wife, Birgit, bought presents for the soldier's children and personally delivered both holiday food and gift-wrapped presents to the home. Another soldier's baby daughter unexpectedly became seriously ill and was admitted to the hospital. Each night, Smith made the hour drive to the soldier's town to keep him and his wife company at the hospital.

Growing up in Tampa, Florida, Paul Ray Smith had been your average American teenager, fond of sports, fast cars, and late-night carousing. After he enlisted right out of Tampa Bay Technical High School, he predictably bristled at the regimentation of Army life, earning his fair share of "extra duty" demerits. But over time the Army worked its special alchemy, turning the base metal of American youth into something stronger and altogether more precious—a band of brothers committed to a cause greater than themselves. While stationed in Germany, Smith met his wife, Birgit, busting a Tom Cruise move out of *Top Gun* by serenading her on their first date with "You've Lost that Loving Feeling." In due course, their children, Jessica and David, were born, and Smith had a family at home as well as in the U.S. Army. By the eve of the Iraq War, his mother, Janice, believed that her son was living his dream, a proud husband and father doing the job he was born for—leading American soldiers.

After clearing Karbala and crossing the Euphrates, 3rd Infantry Division commanders were given their rein, determined to press ahead relentlessly to keep the pressure on the Iraqi Republican Guard. At the front they sensed that Iraqi forces were reacting too slowly to their advance to reposition and effectively counter the U.S. offensive thrust. The commanders decided to push up the assault on Objective Lions by a day, hoping to flank and envelop the Medina Division before it recognized the danger, and thus quickly capture Saddam International Airport, the planned staging area for the upcoming assault on Baghdad. On the downside, the intelligence on the size and disposition of Iraqi defenders at the airport was sketchy.

In its battle rage to reach Baghdad, the 3rd Infantry

Division scorched the landscape black. Burned husks of Iraqi tanks and trucks mounted with antiaircraft guns littered the roadside for miles, each dark smudge of ash and charred detritus along the way bespeaking human drama with a violent end. At random intervals along the way, the metal guardrails of the main highway were crumpled as if from the blows of a giant fist.

As the main force began its siege of Objective Lions, Sergeant Smith and B Company, 11th Engineers began constructing a prisoner-of-war holding area in a courtyard less than a mile from the airport. They were part of a task force occupying blocking positions around the airport perimeter against a possible Iraqi counterattack. The task force had fought for three consecutive days before moving through the night to reach the outskirts of the airport, and while morale remained high, the soldiers were near exhaustion.

The large courtyard was surrounded by high masonry walls flanked by two watchtowers roughly a hundred yards apart that commanded an unobstructed view of the area. The B Company, 2nd Platoon commander was on a reconnaissance mission and absent, leaving Sergeant First Class Smith in charge. After punching a hole in the wall with an earthmover, he posted guards on the perimeter. They quickly reported an estimated fifty enemy soldiers with 60mm mortars and rocket-propelled grenades taking up firing positions nearby. Soon the lead elements of a company-sized force of over a hundred Iraqi Republican Guard troops were visible, and the enemy quickly seized both watchtowers.

Quickly Smith ordered the Bradley Fighting Vehicle and three M113 armored personnel carriers with .50 caliber machine guns to orient on the vulnerable opening in the wall that provided access to the courtyard, and on the watchtowers. Mortar rounds began thumping in the courtyard, followed by the contrails and explosions of rocket-propelled grenades. Through the din, Smith directed his troops to fire toward the vulnerable breach in the wall while personally manning an AT4 antitank weapon and throwing grenades to try to keep the enemy at bay.

Running low on ammunition, the Bradley Fighting Vehicle withdrew to the rear to reload, depriving the defenders of its 25mm chain gun, their heaviest weaponry. Then one of the M113s received a direct mortar hit, seriously wounding three soldiers inside. The Iraqi counterattack was very close to overrunning the task force and collapsing the flank of the U.S. forces besieging the airport.

As he oversaw the evacuation of the wounded, Smith shouted for one of his soldiers to back the damaged armored personnel carrier into the courtyard near the breach in the wall. He jumped into the commander's position atop the vehicle. At that moment Smith and the .50 caliber machine gun were practically all that was standing between the enemy advance and the U.S. task force's vulnerable flank.

"Feed me ammunition whenever you hear the gun get quiet!" Smith shouted to one of his soldiers inside the APC.

As his troops evacuated and regrouped, Smith laid down a steady curtain of machine-gun fire, exposing himself to withering return fire and expending three boxes of lethal .50 caliber ammunition that killed or wounded an estimated thirty to fifty enemy troops. The Iraqi counterattack stalled, and Smith's heroic actions were credited with saving the lives of more than one hundred fellow U.S. soldiers. But his machine gun was finally silenced before a fourth ammo box could be loaded. Smith had been shot in the head and mortally wounded.

Soon after, the soldiers of the 11th Engineer Battalion and the 1st Brigade Combat Team gathered in Iraq to honor their comrade. On top of a two-step platform, the fallen soldier's rifle was buried bayonet-down, his empty boots on the step below. After the chaplain spoke and the formation bowed their heads in silent prayer, a soldier strode before the simple platform of helmet, boots, and rifle for a final roll call and a "missing man" tribute. Three times the soldier's callout was answered with a "Yes, sir!" But not on the fourth call.

"Sergeant Smith!" Silence.

"Sergeant First Class Smith!" Silence.

"Sergeant First Class Paul Ray Smith!"

As if in answer, a bugler blew the first piercing notes of "Taps," the infinitely sad refrain of loss set to music, and all the more poignant for being played so far from home. The "missing man" formation of soldiers wheeled on their heels and marched slowly and forever away without Paul Ray Smith, who would become the first recipient of the Medal of Honor for heroism in the Iraq War.

When they later received their son's belongings, Smith's parents, Donald and Janice, found a letter he had written from Iraq but had never mailed. In it, he told his parents how proud he was of the "privilege to be given 25 of the finest Americans we call Soldiers to lead into war." And then Paul Ray Smith made a pledge to put their welfare first, which he would honor with his life. He was prepared, Smith wrote, "to give all that I am, to ensure that all my boys make it home."

Chapter 3

———★———

No Greater Love

Marine Corps Corporal Jason L. Dunham

The Dunhams were finishing up showering and getting ready to hit the road when Deb walked back into their hotel room and stopped short. Their oldest son, Jason, had graduated from Marine Corps boot camp at Parris Island the previous day, one of the proudest of their lives. The next morning, Jason Dunham was up and showered before first light, and while his parents were in the bathroom, he made their bed and had already taken their suitcases out to the car.

"Where's my suitcase?" Deb asked her son.

"I already packed it," Jason replied.

"Well, please go and get it, I have things I need in there," Deb said, before turning to her husband, Dan, and shaking her head with a smile. The look that passed between the Dunhams said it all: *Who is this polite and attentive young man, and what has he done with Jason?*

Not that Jason Dunham was one to avoid work—far from it. He was the oldest of four siblings who had been raised on a dairy farm in the one-stoplight town of Scio, New York. The family had kept a "chore board" on the wall of their home, and the kids were raised to pitch in and carry their fair share of the workload. Dan Dunham, an Air Force veteran, also worked in the shipping department of a manufacturing company. Deb was a home economics teacher who taught her boys to spell by playing PIG and HORSE with them while shooting baskets. By the time he graduated high school, Jason Dunham was a strapping six-foot-one standout on the Scio High School basketball team.

As a teenager, Jason was a practical joker with an infectious personality. He made friends easily. What most stood out to his family and friends, though, was his genuine kindness and keen sense of right and wrong. One night, he hit a deer with his car, swerving into a woman's yard and tearing it up pretty good. The next day he went back and knocked on her door to make it right. Jason was also extremely protective of his siblings and buddies, and he used his intimidating size and sense of humor to break up or avoid fights. Dan Dunham had drummed into all of his kids that if they ever saw someone weaker in distress, they had a responsibility to help them, no matter the personal cost. Jason had taken that lesson to heart.

In high school, Jason struggled to maintain good enough grades to play sports. As graduation approached, he didn't feel ready for college. Neither of his parents were really surprised when he came home one day with the news that he had met with a Marine recruiter and wanted to join the Marine Corps. The Marines had a reputation for the toughest basic training, and Jason always loved a challenge and competition. His plan was to do one tour and then go to college on the GI Bill. When between his junior and senior years he asked his parents for their consent to join the Marines on a delayed entry program, they willingly signed on the bottom line. The truth was that in their stretch of rural America, if you didn't want to farm or work in a factory, practically the only way out was to go away to college or join the U.S. military.

As a veteran, Dan Dunham knew that the military would teach his son respect and responsibility, but both parents were taken aback by the rapid change the Marine Corps wrought in Jason, part of its time-tested specialty of transforming often self-centered teenagers into a team of warriors. The same kid who couldn't bother to study and was obsessed with sports and girls was suddenly taking classes in history and talking about his military heroes. His intelligence level and maturity were spiking. His athletic frame was becoming even more chiseled.

The transformation was remarkable, as Deb Dunham was fond of recalling.

"The Marine Corps took our boy and polished him into the man he would become," she said.

On the evening of April 13, 2004, Corporal Jason Dunham worked late into the night at the combat operations center of the 3rd Battalion, 7th Marine Regiment. The regiment was stationed in Al-Karabilah, a hardscrabble town near the Syrian border that sat astride a favorite "rat line" that insurgents used to infiltrate into Iraq and smuggle men and weapons down the Euphrates River valley toward Baghdad.

Dunham was shirtless against the oppressive heat, his various tattoos on full display, quietly studying satellite imagery of the route that his Kilo Company would be traveling on an operation the next morning. His diligence and concern for his fellow Marines had already been noted by K Company commanders, who promoted him to squad leader in the 4th Platoon. Fearsome and intimidating drill instructors adorn Marine Corps recruiting posters, but that image belies the traits commanders truly value most in young leaders: an instinct for leading from the front and by example, and a willingness to put the needs of fellow Marines before your own.

Near midnight, Corporal Jason Dunham's squadmates filed into the operations center to bring him an omelet and a cup of juice, and he took a break. They knew the squad leader was burning the midnight oil in order to get tomorrow's mission right and keep them safe. Corporal Dunham never derided green privates fresh out of basic training as "boots" like many of the senior enlisted men did, and when they had rotten jobs to perform like filling sandbags under a broiling sun, the corporal was right by their side. One of the squad members even had a 550-minute phone card in his pocket that Dunham had purchased unbidden so that the cash-strapped Marine could call home and talk to his wife regularly.

All of the squad members also knew that Corporal Dunham had extended his enlistment, which had been due to end the previous July, so that he could stay with his squad through its combat deployment to Iraq. He was determined to bring his Marines home safe. Some of the young Marines thought Dunham was crazy to extend his tour in Iraq, but that's just how Corporal Jason Dunham rolled. And they loved him for it.

★ ★ ★

In fact, the larger intelligence stream flowing into the 3rd Battalion's operation center on April 13, 2004, suggested a volcano on the brink of eruption. Two weeks earlier, four guards from the private contractor Blackwater, all of them former U.S. Special Forces soldiers, had been ambushed in Fallujah, a stronghold for Sunni insurgents a couple of hundred miles down the Euphrates River valley from Al-Karabilah. All four of their bodies had been pulled from their SUV, set on fire and hacked with shovels, then dragged behind cars. Two of them were strung up on beams of a nearby bridge.

After the outrage, the 1st Marine Expeditionary Force in charge of Anbar Province had been ordered to clear Fallujah of insurgents. The Battle of Fallujah then under way was being met with stiff resistance, with heavy casualties on both sides.

As fate would have it, a second uprising of Shiite militias ignited at the same time in Baghdad's Sadr City slums, where the newly arrived U.S. Army 1st Cavalry Division also became involved in an intense urban firefight that claimed heavy casualties. The Sadr City uprising quickly spread to the southern Shiite strongholds of Najaf, Karbala, and al-Hilla. The widespread fighting throughout central Iraq and the lower Euphrates valley threatened to sever the U.S. military's main supply route to Kuwait.

The simultaneous Sunni and Shiite uprisings of April 2004 were a pivotal moment in the Iraq War, amounting to the ultimate "Black Swan" surprise that U.S. military leaders learn to fear. In that shadow, commanders realized for the first time that the strategy of Al Qaeda in Iraq to provoke a civil war that would drive U.S. forces from the country might actually work.

★ ★ ★

On the morning of April 14, Corporal Dunham and his fourteen-man foot patrol passed through the dusty streets of Al-Karabilah. The streets were seemingly calm, but the reconnaissance mission was interrupted when the radio suddenly crackled with reports that the battalion commander's convoy had been hit by a roadside bomb and ambushed nearby. Lieutenant Colonel Matthew Lopez, his translator, and a bodyguard had all reportedly been hit by small-arms fire.

Corporal Dunham and the rest of the patrol jumped into nearby Humvees and raced toward the sound of gunfire. As the convoy approached an arched gateway to the nearby town of Husaybah, a rocket-propelled grenade passed just overhead with a loud whoosh, and the vehicles pulled aside. The patrol split into two fire teams, and the Marines set out on foot to hunt down the insurgents behind the ambush.

Just past noon, Corporal Dunham was, as typical, walking point at the head of the patrol as his squad approached an intersection, his head on a swivel looking for telltale signs of roadside bombs or insurgents. They noted a line of Iraqi pickup trucks and SUVs tucked into an alleyway. The Marines fanned out, approached the convoy, and started searching the vehicles for weapons.

Jason Dunham and Private First Class Kelly Miller

approached a white Toyota Land Cruiser from both the driver and passenger sides. Behind the wheel was an Iraqi man in a black track suit, his eyes darting from side to side. They couldn't see his hands.

Private Miller spotted a rifle sticking out from under a rear floor mat, but when he looked up to warn his partner the Iraqi flung open the door and lunged, grabbing Dunham by the neck. Jason kneed the man in the chest and grappled with him as they both tumbled to the ground. Private Miller raced around from the passenger side and put a chokehold on the insurgent, and Lance Corporal William Hampton ran up to help.

"No, no, no! Watch his hand!" Dunham shouted when he saw the grenade.

In the confusion, none of the other Marines even saw the live grenade roll to the ground at their feet, but Jason Dunham saw it clearly. In an instant he covered the grenade with his Kevlar helmet and then his body to shield his fellow Marines from the blast.

Even muffled, the explosion of the grenade was deafening. Time seemed to slow in the vortex of that blast. As the dust and debris settled, Lance Corporal William Hampton and Private Kelly Miller tried to stagger to their feet. Both Marines were tattered and bleeding from multiple shrapnel wounds. Improbably, the Iraqi insurgent also rose unsteadily to his feet and then ran away. Lance Corporal Jason Sanders, a radio operator who was temporarily deafened by the blast, raised his M16 and fired a burst into the insurgent's back, cutting him down.

They found Jason Dunham lying unconscious, facedown in a pool of his own blood. As his friends lifted him toward the back of a nearby Humvee, Dunham's face was obscured by the blood and his shrapnel wounds. He was recognizable mostly from the tattoo on his chest of an ace of spades and a skull. Beneath him lay strewn pieces of his Kevlar helmet, shredded like paper by the blast.

A medivac helicopter flew Dunham to a nearby shock-trauma platoon coping with ten Marines and a translator from the 3rd Battalion who were also wounded on April 14, 2004. Another medivac helicopter took him up the triage ladder to a hospital at the 7th Marines' base at Al Asad. Doctors found that a grenade fragment had penetrated the left side of his skull just behind his eye, another fragment had entered his brain from the back of his head, and a third had punctured his neck. The dramatic effort to save Dunham's life is captured in great detail by *Wall Street Journal* reporter Michael Phillips in his moving book *The Gift of Valor: A War Story*. Dunham would cling to life for days yet—he was that strong. But Jason Dunham never regained consciousness.

A week later, Dan and Deb Dunham were standing sentry at Jason's bedside when his condition took a turn for the worse. The shrapnel had worked its way down the side of his head, causing irreversible brain damage. Soon his kidneys began failing, and one lung collapsed. Before leaving for Iraq, Jason had asked his father to promise not to leave him on life support if there was no chance of recovery. The time had come for the Dunhams to honor their son's last request.

In those final hours, Marine Corps commandant General Michael Hagee appeared at the bedside and pinned a Purple Heart on Jason's pillow. Deb Dunham cried on the general's shoulder, and then the parents stepped out of the room as doctors disconnected the ventilator. Corporal Jason Dunham died on April 22, 2004, at just twenty-two years of age, having honored his commitment to bring his Marines home alive from Iraq, no matter the personal cost.

In January 2007, President George W. Bush presented Dunham's parents with his posthumous Medal of Honor, the nation's highest award for valor. The White House ceremony marked the first Medal of Honor awarded to a Marine since Vietnam. Memories of Jason Dunham's heroism were recounted, and the tenor of the bittersweet ceremony recalled the New Testament verse *Greater love hath no man than this, that a man lay down his life for his friends.*

Talking to their son's close friends and teammates in Kilo Company before and after the ceremony, the Dunhams sensed the immense burden of survivor's guilt they carried as the beneficiaries of an act of such selfless love. Jason Sanders looked stricken, telling the Dunhams over and over that "I didn't do enough" to save their son, despite his taking out the insurgent who dropped the grenade. The Dunham children went over to Sanders after the ceremony to deliver a message: You don't understand—you are our hero for making sure that the insurgent didn't kill more Marines.

Corporal Billy Hampton thought about Jason Dunham's heroism on his behalf every day, and he had the scars of multiple shrapnel wounds to remind him. He was polite at the ceremony, but the Dunhams could tell he was uncomfortable, calling them Jason's "poor mom and dad." Hampton would later grow close to Jason's kid brother Kyle.

Private Kelly Miller had been one of Jason's closest friends in the company, and he suffered the worst from survivor's guilt. He would call the Dunhams later to say he had been asked to attend another ceremony honoring Dunham as a Medal of Honor recipient, but he could barely bring himself to go.

"I told him that he didn't have to attend, and Kelly thanked me," Deb Dunham said in an interview with the author. "He needed to heal and work through his life in his own way. It was difficult to explain to these amazing men that God has a plan, and this was what Jason was meant to do. They had a hard time coming to grips with that because the Marine code of honor is that you always have your buddy's back."

After his surgeries and physical therapy, Corporal Kelly Miller would return for another deployment to Iraq. When his mother asked him why, Miller told her, "I have to go and finish what Dunham started, and bring my guys home."

To help keep Jason's memory alive, Deb Dunham and her daughter serve as a sponsor and maid of honor, respectively, to the USS *Jason Dunham*, a U.S. Navy destroyer named in his honor. Both parents also keep in touch with his former Kilo Company teammates to check in on their lives and assure them that Jason would want them to be happy and guilt-free.

"These young men who were so close to Jason still carry the burden of his death," Dan Dunham said. "And we try and tell them that it's all good. I know, because Jason has come and seen me a few times to let me know. I'm not a religious person, but I can tell you that that kid has come and seen me a few times."

Chapter 4

—★—

House of Broken Mirrors

Army Staff Sergeant David G. Bellavia

The night was pitch dark and the garbage-strewn streets of Fallujah deserted and ghostly as U.S. Army soldiers went house-to-house hunting a band of jihadists. Though exhausted by three days of nearly nonstop operations, "Alpha 2-2"—Alpha Company, 2nd Battalion, 2nd Infantry Regiment, of the 1st Infantry Division—was a crack unit, with a reputation for discipline and doggedness. Team members had already seen combat in the battles for Najaf, Mosul, Baqubah, and Muqdadiyah. That kind of nose for action never went searching in vain for long, not in Iraq circa 2004.

The nearly three hundred thousand citizens of Fallujah had largely abandoned the city to a few thousand jihadists and insurgents who had booby-trapped and fortified many of its buildings, connecting them with underground tunnels for clandestine reinforcement or retreat as the situation demanded. Many of the insurgents fortified themselves not only with stockpiles of weapons, but also with amphetamines and other drugs to make them nearly impervious to pain and fear. Their goal was to lure the American soldiers into close combat and a relative knife fight in the dark that negated the U.S. military's advantage in long-range weapons and standoff fire.

All of which made house clearing an especially harrowing mission. Alpha 2-2 had thus developed a countertactic. An M1 Abrams tank would fire a high-explosive 120mm round into the front door, followed by a Bradley Fighting Vehicle clearing rooms with windows opening onto the street with its powerful 25mm chain gun. Only then would infantry squad "dismounts" enter and clear the building.

Yet by the time that First Lieutenant Joaquin Meno and his 3rd Platoon arrived at the tenth house on the block, the order had come down that the M1 could not fire in the direction of these buildings because of the danger to friendly forces operating in the area. Then the Bradley's chain gun jammed. Staff Sergeant Colin Fitts—a legendary soldier in the unit who had been shot three separate times earlier in the deployment yet refused to abandon the fight—nevertheless led his men into the foul-smelling darkness.

In a well-practiced series of covering moves as intricate as a drill team, the squad moved quickly through a narrow foyer and into a larger living room. A doorway on the other side led down a hallway toward a stairwell. The lead soldier turned to enter the hallway and a metallic sound prompted his sergeant to pull him aside by his battle webbing just as the room exploded with the jackhammer report from two belt-fed machine guns positioned behind a blast wall beneath the staircase. The sound in the close confines was deafening.

Soldiers dove for cover as high-velocity rounds ripped through walls and splintered woodwork. Shards of glass and bits of plaster peppered their faces. Strobe lights mounted on weapons careened around the room and bounced crazily off the ceiling as everyone hugged the walls and searched for targets. Carefully rehearsed tactics flew out the window with that first volley, and in the pandemonium that ensued the entire squad realized it was pinned down and trapped.

"We're all gonna die!" one of the U.S. soldiers shouted.

On any given day, a U.S. infantry unit in combat will witness multiple acts of conspicuous gallantry that would confound most observers. Combat forges iron bonds of devotion among soldiers who must repeatedly risk their lives to protect each other. So the outcome of a given firefight can depend on who the charged electricity of combat ignites first, short-circuiting the survival instinct that would normally shut a man down before he rushes a machine gun. On November 10, 2004, that man was Staff Sergeant David Bellavia.

After a round disabled his M16 rifle, Bellavia grabbed an M249 Squad Automatic Weapon (SAW) in the chaos, and then exposed himself to the enemy's hail of bullets, spraying automatic fire repeatedly at the enemy position and suppressing the machine-gun bunker long enough for his team to escape the house. Finally, the SAW ran out of ammunition. When the hammer clicked down on an empty chamber, Bellavia scrambled out of the house as bullets whistled all around. None of his teammates doubted that he had just saved their lives.

Remarkably, the acts of extreme valor that would make David Bellavia the first living recipient of the Medal of Honor for actions during the Iraq War had only just begun.

★ ★ ★

Operation Phantom Fury, which was designed to clear Fallujah of insurgents in November 2004, was a battle long foretold. From the earliest days of the Iraq invasion the U.S. presence in the hardscrabble Sunni stronghold and Baathist redoubt had seemed cursed. In April 2003, soldiers from the 82nd Airborne, believing they were taking incoming fire, had opened fire on a crowd of protesters in the city center, reportedly killing seventeen and wounding more than seventy locals. A year later, insurgents in Fallujah ambushed four American security contractors, leaving their bodies to an angry crowd that literally ripped them apart and hung them from a bridge span.

After that outrage, civilian leadership in the U.S. Coalition Provision Authority ordered U.S. Marines to clear Fallujah of insurgents, and then in the middle of the battle reversed course in the face of a public backlash and a general uprising throughout Iraq. The Marines were told to do something that ran counter to every instinct drummed into them from the moment they first set foot on Parris Island: to stand down in the face of a determined enemy.

U.S. commanders rightly predicted at the time that the perceived retreat only delayed a day of reckoning in Fallujah. In the months that followed, Fallujah—a trading hub on the banks of the Euphrates River west of Baghdad, and a favored way station for foreign fighters following "rat lines" of infiltration into Iraq from Syria—had become a permissive operating base for a witches' brew of Sunni insurgent and terrorist groups. They included archterrorist Abu Musab al-Zarqawi and his Al Qaeda in Iraq, which used Fallujah as a base to assemble car and truck bombs that it deployed to devastating effect in mass casualty bombings targeting Shiite civilians in and around Baghdad. The tactic was pushing Iraq toward all-out sectarian civil war.

In early November 2004, a coalition force of some 13,500 U.S. Marines, Army soldiers, and British and Iraqi counterparts was poised to finish the job of pacifying Fallujah. Standing in their way were an estimated 3,000 insurgents who had spent months digging tunnels, fortifying trenches and bunkers, and booby-trapping buildings in an otherwise largely deserted city. U.S. commanders in Iraq didn't know it at the time, but Operation Phantom Fury would spark the bloodiest urban fighting that American troops had experienced since the Battle of Hue in Vietnam during the 1968 Tet Offensive.

Crouching beneath a low wall on the outside of the insurgent house and trying to catch his breath, Sergeant Bellavia made a mental head count to make sure everyone had made it out alive. The situation on the darkened street was chaotic. He could tell from the radio that his Alpha Company commander, Captain Sean Sims, was engaged in an intense fight elsewhere in the city that was taking priority in terms of air and fire support. Meanwhile, his team was taking insurgent fire from the surrounding rooftops and dispersing to try and neutralize that threat.

A surge of thoughts and emotions raced through Bellavia's

head. The adrenaline was still pumping from the fear and excitement of the firefight. He was also angry that the insurgents inside that house had tried to kill his closest friends, and that they had dared to contest the U.S. Army on the field of battle. He had seen rocket-propelled grenades stacked on the inside of the house that still represented a serious threat to his team. Most of all, Bellavia felt a profound sense of letdown. He had come face-to-face with a determined enemy, and he had been the one forced to break contact and retreat.

Bellavia had grown up in the small town of Lyndonville, New York, the son of a successful dentist and the youngest of four boys. He remembered listening as a boy to the vivid stories of his grandfather Joseph Brunacini, who had served in World War II during the Normandy campaign and earned a Bronze Star for valor. Those stories first planted the idea that the life of an Army infantryman was one of purpose and nobility. In 1999, Bellavia had enlisted in the Army to follow that dream. After the 9/11 terror attacks, he knew with certainty that the story of his own war had begun.

As he crouched behind the wall and gathered his thoughts, Bellavia made a decision that would astound his fellow soldiers, though few even knew about it at the time. First, he established a cordon of fire on the outside of the house with his SAW gunners to block any insurgent retreat, and then he instructed a Bradley Fighting Vehicle that had just arrived on scene to fire its 25mm cannon into the house's windows. Then, with just Staff Sergeant Scott Lawson as backup, Bellavia reentered the stronghold to confront the band of jihadists inside.

✳ ✳ ✳

The house was pitch black and eerily quiet when Sergeant Bellavia entered through the front doorway, and it looked somehow different. The Bradley's high-explosive rounds had reconfigured the furniture. At least the insurgents knew the American soldiers hadn't forgotten about them.

Alone except for Sergeant Lawson to his rear, Bellavia noticed details that had escaped him in the crowded chaos of their initial ambush. He was sloshing through nearly ankle-deep water from burst water pipes, the slime clinging to his boots and the overwhelming smell of sewage and garbage an assault on his senses. There were bits of broken mirrors on many of the walls and floors, reflecting rooms at strange angles and giving the place an evil haunted house vibe. With almost no illumination to work with, the night-vision goggles created a "cat's eye" effect of extreme tunnel vision.

From the corner of his eye Bellavia saw movement in a broken piece of mirror, and then the face of an insurgent in the next room was reflected staring back at him. Without even aiming, he thrust his 40mm grenade launcher around the corner of a doorway and fired into the room, the round shooting out through the back of the house harmlessly. The insurgent was loading up an RPG, but his movement was constrained by the broken furniture. Bellavia advanced, aimed his rifle, and puts rounds on him until the man collapsed.

Bellavia had already tossed his radio because it would have given away his position. He stopped and listened and waited until he saw movement in a doorway as a second insurgent passed. Bellavia got the jump on him too, firing and hitting him. Yet when he swung back around a few seconds later the man's body was nowhere to be seen.

Sergeant Bellavia's mind was playing tricks on him. He wasn't sure if he'd just shot the insurgent who'd initially run into the kitchen, or some new enemy who had been in hiding. The reality wasn't like the movies, where you shoot a bad guy, they fall, and then that's the end of it. In this cursed building, they dropped and then seemed to disappear. In the tense silence he heard the patter of footsteps somewhere in the three-story house. Some of them sounded like they were coming from behind where Sergeant Lawson was supposed to be guarding his back. Bellavia swung his rifle around to meet this new threat and was startled to see *Time* magazine reporter Michael Ware. *Jesus!*

Bellavia had worked with embedded reporters before and generally had no time for them. But he had never met a reporter who was willing to put himself in the middle of a house fight. In that moment his estimation of Ware shot way up, especially after the reporter ran back outside to call for help and reinforcements for Bellavia.

As he advanced into the house a "ghost round" whizzed through the room, and Bellavia swung toward the staircase, where another insurgent was coming down the stairs aiming an AK-47. Taking cover behind the wall, Bellavia noticed a gap of a few inches between the doorframe and the concrete wall. He aimed the rifle barrel through the gap and fired until the insurgent crumpled.

Just then a wardrobe in the room to his rear flew open and another insurgent came stumbling out as the wardrobe toppled to the floor nearly at Bellavia's feet. The insurgent tried to make it to the door while firing blindly behind him with a snub-nosed AK-47, the bullets striking the wall and the wardrobe, which Bellavia was using for cover. The insurgent stepped over a mattress and lost his footing, toppling into the water. Sergeant Bellavia saw his chance and put rounds into the insurgent, who somehow managed to scramble out the door and up the stairs.

Bellavia tried to give chase up the staircase but his boots were slick from the foul water. After stepping on a smeared trail of blood he toppled down on his face. Just then a round exploded on the wall where his head had just been. Bellavia managed to throw a fragmentation grenade into the room at the top of the stairs, and then crouched for cover. When the reverberation and dust from the explosion subsided, he heard the wounded insurgent shouting in Arabic to someone on the third floor. Whatever they were talking about, Bellavia knew it couldn't be good. He had to break up their conversation.

Entering the room at the top of the stairs, he was immediately grabbed by the wounded insurgent. They wrestled and Bellavia put a chokehold on the man to try and keep him from giving away their position. The jihadist fought furiously despite his wounds, biting into Sergeant Bellavia's arm and then smacking him in the face with the butt of an AK-47. In the desperate grapple, Bellavia grabbed his knife and slit the man's throat.

Utterly spent from the fighting and carnage, Bellavia set down his rifle and removed his helmet. Then he walked out on a second-story patio as if in a trance to smoke a cigarette. Killing the last insurgent in hand-to-hand combat had taken everything he had left. "I was just stressed out, and I was thinking, 'I'm going to have this cigarette outside on this patio, and my guys are going to come in and we're going to take out this last guy as a unit,'" he recounted in an interview. "Because I just had too much."

At that moment, a fifth jihadist leapt down from the third floor and landed on the patio practically at Sergeant Bellavia's feet. Luckily, he landed awkwardly and rolled on the floor before he could get the drop with his rifle. Bellavia grabbed his own rifle first and shot the insurgent point-blank. As the man tried to crawl to the edge of the rooftop patio he fell, toppling into the darkness of the courtyard below. Minutes later, Bellavia's Alpha 2-2 teammates burst into the room, having followed the trail of blood and carnage inside the house to this final chamber of horrors.

★ ★ ★

Staff Sergeant David Bellavia left the Army the next year, but he was driven by a restlessness that was not unusual for veterans of the "forever wars" in Iraq and Afghanistan. When a soldier's war never ends, it sometimes feels like they should be back in the fight. Bellavia thus returned to Iraq in 2006 and 2007 to cover continued heavy fighting there as an embedded reporter. In 2007, he wrote a book about his experiences in Fallujah, entitled *House to House*. He would later run unsuccessfully for Congress, and he went on to host a successful radio show in Buffalo, New York.

On learning early in 2019 that he would receive the Medal of Honor for his actions in Fallujah so long ago, David Bellavia decided to use the platform to spread a message of teamwork and national unity that he had lived as a soldier. In a country more politically divided than at any time in its modern history, with his countrymen and -women seemingly most eager to fight each other, he felt there was hope in the example of Alpha 2-2.

"There's a million-plus reasons why Americans are divided right now, and throughout our history we've always disagreed and dissented, but we always found a way to put our differences aside and focus on what's best for the nation when it counted most," he said. That sense of common purpose is the foundation of the U.S. Army, he noted, calling it "the world's largest adoption agency."

"We don't care if your dad died and left you millions of dollars or not. I personally never cared what God a soldier worshipped, what color they are, or who they loved," said Bellavia in an interview. "If someone is willing to get shot at for me and my buddy, I will lead or follow you anywhere. At the end of the day, I believe our country is worthy of that kind of sacrifice."

As he stood in uniform in the White House on Wednesday, June 26, 2019, to receive the Medal of Honor from President Donald Trump, former staff sergeant David Bellavia called onto the stage the many members of his unit who served together in Iraq and were present at the White House ceremony, along with members of the Gold Star families of the soldiers the unit lost in the Battle of Fallujah. They were among the thirty-seven soldiers who made the ultimate sacrifice during the brigade's year in Iraq. All told it was a crowded stage in the East Room.

Anticipating the moment earlier in the week, Bellavia admitted thinking about the fallen every day. "They gave up all their tomorrows for us, so I'm very proud to be part of the generation of Iraq War veterans who met and at times surpassed the highest standards of American warrior tradition," he said. "Seeing all these guys after fifteen years—I just have so much love. I never thought I'd find love on a battlefield. That experience is ghastly and ghoulish. But you see people doing things for each other that they would never, ever do in any other circumstance. Let me tell you it is a sight to see, and it will change your life forever."

Chapter 5

———☆———

The Valley of Shadow

Navy Lieutenant (SEAL) Michael P. Murphy

What do you think we should do, Axe?" Lieutenant Michael Murphy asked Petty Officer Matthew Axelson, a member of his four-man SEAL reconnaissance team.

The subject at hand was three Afghan goat herders, one no more than a young teenager by the look of him, who had stumbled onto their hideaway deep behind Taliban lines, high in the Hindu Kush.

"I think we should kill them, because we can't let them go," Axelson replied, and the strictly military logic of his answer was obvious to them all.

The SEAL team was perched at the end of a granite finger of rock on a steep mountain ridge. The spot offered an excellent view of the mountain village far below where their target was thought to be staying. There was only one trail onto the overlook, and one way out. If the scowling Afghan goat herders gave away their position to the local Taliban warlord they were hunting, Ahmad Shah and his hardened band of some eighty to two hundred "Mountain Tigers" would surely come running. Not only would their surveillance mission be compromised, but the four-man SEAL team, which had lost radio contact with headquarters, might never make it off that ten-thousand-foot mountain alive.

"And you, Danny?" Murphy asked Petty Officer Danny Dietz, his radioman.

"I don't really give a shit what we do. You want me to kill

them, I'll kill 'em. Just give me the word," Dietz replied. "I only work here."

"Marcus?" Lieutenant Murphy asked Petty Officer Marcus Luttrell, a medic and one of his snipers. Luttrell later captured their predicament in gripping detail in his bestselling book *Lone Survivor*, which recalls their conversation over the fateful decision.

"Well, until right now I'd assumed killing 'em was our only option. I'd like to hear what you think, Murph," Luttrell answered.

Just a few years earlier, twenty-nine-year-old Michael Murphy, fondly called "Murph" by his family and friends, had been headed to law school. He had already been accepted to several schools after graduating with honors from Penn State University with not one but two bachelor of arts degrees, in psychology and political science. A Long Island boy who grew up in the New York City commuter town of Patchogue, Murphy was an excellent athlete, playing ice hockey in college and working as a lifeguard during summer breaks. After his college graduation he seemed destined for a promising career in law.

Then Murphy attended a SEAL mentoring session at the U.S. Merchant Marine Academy at Kings Point, New York, and a fire was kindled deep inside that few had seen coming. At that moment, his life took an unexpected detour that led improbably to a rocky escarpment high in the mountains of Afghanistan, where he confronted a decision that was the tactical equivalent of "Sophie's Choice."

"Listen, if we kill them, someone will find their bodies real quick," Murphy explained to his team, nodding at the small herd of goats baying all around them. "And when these guys don't get home for their dinner, their friends and relatives are going to head straight out to look for them, especially this fourteen-year-old. The main problem is the goats. Because they can't be hidden, and that's where people will look."

Murphy could seemingly see it all clearly, as Luttrell recalled in *Lone Survivor*. "When they find the bodies, the Taliban leaders will sing to the Afghan media. The media in the U.S.A. will latch on to it and write stuff about the brutish U.S. Armed Forces. Very shortly after that, we'll be charged with murder. The murder of innocent unarmed Afghan farmers."

Murphy could have pulled rank, but that wasn't his way. All of their lives hung in the balance, so he put it to a vote.

"Axe?" he asked again.

"We're not murderers no matter what we do. We're on active duty behind enemy lines, sent here by our senior commanders. We have a right to do everything we can to save our own lives," said Axelson, holding his ground. "The military decision is obvious. To turn them loose would be wrong."

"Danny?" Murphy asked.

"As before. I don't give a shit what you decide," Dietz told his team leader. "Just tell me what to do."

"Marcus? Call it."

Luttrell looked at the three Afghan herders, the scowls on their face plain to read. But a voice from his Christian conscience whispered in the back of his mind that it would be wrong to kill unarmed civilians in cold blood, just the same.

"We got to let 'em go," he said.

"Okay, I guess that's two votes to one. Danny abstains," noted Lieutenant Murphy. "We gotta let 'em go."

★ ★ ★

The surveillance and reconnaissance mission to stalk and pinpoint Ahmad Shah, and, if possible, to capture or kill him, was straight out of the SEAL handbook. By June 2005, the main U.S. military effort in the global war on terror had shifted to Iraq, and the Taliban and Al Qaeda forces that had been so decisively routed in 2001 were regrouping along the border between Afghanistan and Pakistan, where they enjoyed sanctuary. Few of the loose-knit Afghan guerrilla groups that traveled under the Taliban banner were deadlier or more experienced than Shah's Mountain Tigers, who traveled and recruited among the high mountain villages east of Asadabad. They were experts at ambushes, and already had the blood of numerous U.S. Marines on their hands.

Yet Operation Red Wings to fix Shah's location and maybe get off a "kill shot" was shrouded in uncertainty. The mission had been called off at the last minute numerous times as the intelligence about Shah's likely whereabouts shifted. He was a cagey operator in his midthirties who grew up in these mountains and never stayed in one location for long, and his band of fighters exhibited the kind of fieldcraft gained from many years of guerrilla operations.

What worried the SEAL team was the lack of detailed

intelligence and the terrain. The high mountain village they were to scout had more than two dozen buildings, but they had no idea in which Ahmad Shah was staying, and they only had a grainy photograph to identify him. Satellite photographs of the area also revealed steep cliffs with very little vegetation on the mountainsides above the village, meaning concealment would be difficult. There were few places to hide, and a small army of local fighters to hide from.

Under the circumstances, goat herders stumbling into their hideout in broad daylight was the worst kind of misfortune. The fact that the SEAL team had lost radio communication at that moment, and thus had no guidance from higher headquarters, compounded the rotten luck. They were on their own, and as they watched the released goat herders disappear up the mountain Lieutenant Michael Murphy wasn't going to sit around and wait to see if their luck turned.

"What now?" Danny Dietz asked him.

"Move in five," Murphy said, gathering up equipment.

The new hideaway was on a ledge on the mountain wall, some forty or fifty yards from the summit, with a group of trees and some large boulders for concealment. From the top, it would be nearly impossible to see the four camouflaged SEAL commandos, who had spread out in defensive positions. The sun beat down, and at nearly the two-hour mark since the goat herders had crested the mountain, Murphy joked in a whisper that he was going to stroll down to the village to see about borrowing a phone. And then he made a shushing sound that they all understood as a warning.

Straight above their heads on the crest of the hill were the silhouettes of scores of heavily armed Taliban fighters. They couldn't have seen the SEAL team, but the guerrillas knew the terrain, and immediately began to scramble down the mountainside to the left and right flanks of their position. The SEAL team was trapped.

A Taliban fighter pointing an AK-47 rifle appeared from behind a tree just twenty yards above their position, peering into the shadows. Petty Officer Marcus Luttrell was the first to fire, killing the Afghan with a head shot. As he describes it in *Lone Survivor*, at that moment all hell broke loose. "The Taliban unleashed an avalanche of gunfire at us, straight down the mountain, from every angle."

For many minutes the SEALs engaged the Taliban guerrillas in a fierce firefight, killing and wounding many of them but in constant danger of being overrun by the enemy's overwhelming numbers. Unable to move forward up the mountain and about to be flanked, Lieutenant Murphy ordered them to retreat down the steep mountainside to their rear.

"Fall back!" he shouted.

Both Murphy and Luttrell tumbled head over heels down the steep slope, picking up speed and trying desperately to grab hold of trees or bushes to check their fall. They catapulted over the lip of a narrow ledge and plunged down the steep slope some two hundred yards before landing with bone-shaking thuds in a patch of more level ground. They were both battered but somehow still alive, within arm's reach of their weapons, but Murphy was bleeding from a bullet wound in his stomach.

A rocket-propelled grenade landed close by, and they both scrambled through the dust and smoke to take cover behind two felled trees. They immediately began firing again at the Taliban fighters streaming down the mountainside, who were once again trying to flank the American commandos. Someone had trained them well in battlefield tactics.

Through the smoke and din of battle both Murphy and Luttrell saw another body cartwheeling down the mountain, flipping over the ledge above and crashing down the steep slope. Petty Officer Matthew Axelson also somehow survived the fall and the enemy incoming, and he leapt over the logs to join his teammates. Soon Petty Officer Dietz came careening down the mountain, only when he landed with a thud he didn't get up. Axelson gave them covering fire as Murphy and Luttrell broke into the clearing and dragged Dietz behind the felled trees. Dietz struggled into a firing crouch, despite the fact that a Taliban bullet had blown off his right thumb. Luttrell had been stripped of all of his medical supplies in the fall down the mountain, and he could do little to treat the wounds of his friends.

Once again, the four SEALs fought furiously to avoid being flanked. Despite heavy enemy losses they were losing ground to the overwhelming numbers of Taliban fighters. Once again Lieutenant Murphy acted before they were surrounded or overrun.

"They'll kill us all if we stay here! Jump, guys, for fuck's sake, jump!" Luttrell recalled him shouting.

Murphy leapt over the nearby precipice, followed quickly by his teammates. All four commandos landed in a thicket of bushes some thirty or forty feet below, falling practically on top of each other. They staggered up and spread out once again to assume new firing positions as the Taliban fighters scrambled down the mountain after them.

The SEALs were hemmed in by sheer granite walls on three sides. Bullets and grenade shrapnel ricocheted off the stones and zinged through air heavy with the smell of cordite. Danny Dietz was shot again in the small of his back, his mouth falling open as he gurgled blood. He continued to fire until he was shot yet again through the neck, whereupon he dropped his rifle and slumped to the ground.

When Luttrell dragged him to the rock face for cover, Dietz propped himself up against the mountain and somehow resumed firing. And once again Lieutenant Murphy made the call before they could be flanked.

"Fall back!" Murphy shouted.

After a roughly fifteen-foot fall off the rock ledge down to a streambed, the battered and bloody SEAL team members staggered to their feet and once again assumed defensive fire positions. They blasted away straight up the mountain at point-blank range, cutting down Taliban fighters just twenty to thirty yards away and taking withering incoming. Danny Dietz took another bullet at the base of his neck and fell to the ground, bleeding from five gunshot wounds. Marcus Luttrell ran to him and was dragging Dietz toward cover when a Taliban fighter appeared out of the rocks to the right with a dead bead on them with his AK-47. Matthew Axelson dropped the Afghan guerrilla with two shots to the head.

Luttrell and Dietz had barely reached the cover of the rock face when Axelson was hit in the chest, dropping his rifle and slumping to the ground. In a supreme act of will, Axelson struggled back to his feet a few moments later and resumed firing.

For the fourth time in the hourlong firefight, the Taliban nearly had the SEAL team surrounded, and once again Lieutenant Murphy told them to fall back down the escarpment to their rear. Luttrell was dragging Danny Dietz and bringing up the rear when a bullet caught his friend in the face, ending his terrible suffering.

By the time the three surviving SEALs regrouped, they were once again pinned down and in danger of being flanked. Rocket-propelled grenades were whistling in on white phosphorus smoke trails, their explosions shaking the nearby trees and sending the waters of the stream spilling over its banks. Given their serious wounds and the far superior numbers of the enemy, the situation was all but hopeless. The Taliban fighters were screaming at them in their strange tongue from just up the mountain, and the SEAL commandos yelled right back.

"Fuck surrender," Murphy shouted, his voice rising about the din of battle. "Remember, we're never out of the fight!"

The incoming fire intensified. Mike Murphy was shot through the chest, but somehow still continued to return fire.

Then Axelson was hit in the head, and Marcus Luttrell helped him slump down behind a rock for cover. When he turned back around, his team leader and friend did an almost unfathomable thing.

Lieutenant Michael Murphy pulled his mobile phone from his pocket, walked away from the cliff wall and out into the middle of the clearing to get reception, then sat on a small rock and dialed back to headquarters.

"My men are taking heavy fire…we're getting picked apart. My guys are dying out here. We need help," Murphy said into his phone, knowing it was the only chance to save his two teammates. Just then he was shot through the back, the impact causing blood to spurt from his chest wound and making him drop the phone and his rifle. Then Murphy braced himself, retrieved both, and once again put the phone to his ear.

"Roger that, sir," he signed off. "Thank you."

Lieutenant Michael "Murph" Murphy continued to fight, but he soon succumbed to his many wounds, and his position was overrun by the Taliban fighters. Petty Officer Matthew "Axe" Axelson also died of his wounds on that mountain deep in the Hindu Kush, not far from where his friend and teammate Petty Officer Danny Dietz fell.

Remarkably, a rocket-propelled grenade blasted Petty Officer Marcus Luttrell over the ridge where the team had made its last stand, knocking him unconscious. Badly wounded, he would travel seven miles while being hunted by the Taliban fighters, at times crawling through the mountains on his hands and knees to relieve the pain in his shrapnel-shredded legs. In his stirring account of the ordeal, Luttrell recalls imagining that his three teammates and friends were still alive and covering his back, as he desperately clung to the message in the "Psalm of the SEALs," the one repeated at all of their religious services and funerals:

Yea, though I walk through the valley of the shadow of death, I will fear no evil. Thou art with me; Thy rod and Thy staff comfort me...

Unbeknownst to Marcus Luttrell, the shadow that descended over the U.S. Special Forces community that day was even darker than he imagined. Alerted to their dire situation, an MH-47 Chinook helicopter was launched carrying a quick reaction force of eight additional SEAL commandos and eight Army Special Forces soldiers. Driven by the need of their wounded and surrounded brothers in arms, and Lieutenant Murphy's haunting words that "my guys are dying out here...we need help," the QRF commanders attempted a risky daylight insertion into hazardous enemy territory during an ongoing firefight. As the massive Chinook tilted back for the fast-rope insertion of the force, a Taliban gunner fired a rocket-propelled grenade through the rear of the helicopter, igniting its fuel tanks. The Chinook smashed into the mountainside in a fiery ball, killing all sixteen Special Forces troops aboard; the fallen SEALs were Lieutenant Commander Eric Kristensen, Lieutenant Mike McGreevy Jr., Senior Chief Dan Healy, Chief Jacques Fontan, and Petty Officers Jeff Lucas, Jeff Taylor, James Suh, and Shane Patton; the Army "Night Stalkers" of the 120th Special Operations Aviation Regiment lost were Major Steve Reich, Chief Warrant Officers

Chris Scherkenbach and Corey Goodnature, Master Sergeant James Ponder, Sergeants First Class Marcus Muralles and Mike Russell, Staff Sergeant Shamus Goare, and Sergeant Kip Jacoby. Their deaths made June 28, 2005, the deadliest single day in six years of fighting in Afghanistan, and the worst for the Special Forces community since World War II.

Eventually, Marcus Luttrell was aided by Afghan villagers who took him in and gave him shelter. Several times the Taliban came to the village and demanded that the American be turned over, but the villagers steadfastly refused, honoring the ancient Pashtun tribal code of Pashtunwali, which preaches hospitality toward strangers. One of the villagers carried a note from Luttrell to a U.S. Marine outpost, and U.S. forces launched an operation to rescue the lone American survivor of the Battle of Murphy's Ridge.

Lieutenant Michael Murphy's posthumous Medal of Honor cites his "undaunted courage, intrepid fighting spirit and inspirational devotion to his men in the face of certain death," enabling him to "relay the position of his unit, an act that ultimately led to the rescue of Luttrell and the recovery of the remains of the three who were killed in the battle."

"Was there ever a greater SEAL team commander than Mikey, an officer who fought to the last and, as perhaps his dying move, risked everything to save his remaining men?" Luttrell concludes in *Lone Survivor*. "If they built a memorial to him as high as the Empire State Building, it would never be high enough for me."

Chapter 6

———★———

A Meaningful Life

Army Staff Sergeant Jared C. Monti

For days the patrol walked in the dim twilight, scrambling up goat trails, crossing cold mountain streams, and picking their way across rocky hillsides in the near dark. They moved at dusk or early dawn to avoid detection and the relentless glare of the sun. By midday the temperatures had soared to nearly 100 degrees, and the team of forward observers, scouts, and snipers hunkered down under the cover of trees and bushes, keeping their long-range scopes trained on the mountain village far below. Somewhere down there was the summer residence of insurgent leader and local warlord Hadji Usman, who was high on the task force's target list. Their mission was to scout the valley below in advance of a major operation to clear this area near the Afghan-Pakistan border of militants.

The team were members of the 3rd Squadron, 7th Cavalry Regiment of the 10th Mountain Division. The light infantry division was formed during World War II and manned primarily by lumberjacks, forest rangers, wilderness guides, and members of the National Ski Patrol. In other words, by any recruit who felt at home in the mountains. The 10th Mountain fought with distinction in the mountains of northern Italy and Austria in 1945, and by the summer of 2006 it was on its way to becoming the single most deployed unit in the post-9/11 wars in Afghanistan and Iraq.

After a three-day trek through the mountains, leaders Staff Sergeant Jared Monti and Staff Sergeant Christopher

Cunningham halted the sixteen-man patrol on a flat outcropping atop a narrow ridge. At the northern edge of the clearing was a line of trees and dense bushes, and toward the southern end several small boulders and remnants of an old stone wall. The position had decent cover, and it offered commanding views of the Gremen Valley and the village of Gowardesh some three thousand feet below. The team leaders decided to make camp for the night.

As they finished their Meals, Ready-to-Eat (MREs) and their remaining water, some of the younger soldiers gravitated toward thirty-year-old Staff Sergeant Monti, whom they fondly nicknamed "Grandpa." Monti had been a championship wrestler and triathlete in high school, and he had already notched a deployment to Korea and an earlier combat tour to Afghanistan, receiving a Bronze Star and Army Commendation Medal for valor. His father, Paul, was a teacher, and his mother, Janet, a nurse, and they had instilled in their son a love of mentorship and sense of compassion that perfectly befit a noncommissioned officer leading young soldiers in combat. Jared Monti called them "his boys," and he was exactly the kind of experienced and attentive leader you would want on a dangerous mission deep in enemy territory.

The next morning, headquarters radioed that the main assault had been delayed for several days. That left the patrol in a precarious position. They were already low on food, water, and batteries, and had expected to be resupplied under the cover of the major air assault, when U.S. helicopters would be swarming all over the valley. Now a single helicopter resupply mission was launched that could draw attention to their position on the ridgeline. But there was nothing to be done about it.

Sergeants Monti and Cunningham led ten of their soldiers down to the resupply drop zone at midday. Soon the UH-60 Black Hawk helicopter appeared over the ridgeline and swept in to drop off the food and water. Within minutes the twelve supply-laden soldiers were trudging back up the mountainside to the observation position. A smaller group of four soldiers had remained behind to continue surveying the valley.

As soon as they reentered the clearing, Specialist Max Noble, the patrol's medic, waved the patrol leaders over.

"We're being watched," he told them.

"What do you mean, we're being watched?" asked Sergeant John Hawes, alarmed.

Specialist Noble handed over the spotting scope and pointed down the mountain. Through the scope they could clearly see an Afghan man looking up toward their position on the ridgeline through military-style binoculars. That was a bad sign. Villagers typically didn't possess expensive high-powered binoculars. As Sergeant Hawes noted, birdwatching is not a popular pastime in the hardscrabble mountain villages. After a few minutes the Afghan man stood up and gathered a light bag, then disappeared into a draw heading uphill.

Dusk was fast approaching, and the patrol was uneasy. The leaders set up a security perimeter and scheduled guard rotations throughout the night. Six of the soldiers positioned themselves at the northern end of the clearing near the trees and dense foliage. Four others lay along the trail on the eastern edge of the position, occasionally using their spotting scopes to monitor the valley below. Sergeants Monti, Cunningham, and Hawes huddled behind the boulders on the southern end of the clearing. They talked about doubling the guard shift after being compromised. It was already 6:45 in the evening and the shadows were lengthening on the mountainside. Everyone felt a bit shaky.

At the northern end of the clearing, Specialist Franklin Woods thought he heard something. It sounded like the shuffling of feet in the nearby woods. Before he could raise the alarm, rocket-propelled grenades whizzed overhead, and two medium machine guns opened up from somewhere above along with a fusillade of small-arms fire from the nearby tree line.

The suddenness and intensity of the incoming fire scattered the exposed soldiers nearest to the trees and along the eastern edge of the trail. Specialist John Garner reached for his rifle only to have a machine-gun bullet rip it from his hands. Other soldiers who had put their rifles down to eat scrambled back to the boulders for cover unarmed. Specialist Shawn Heistand and Private Brian Bradbury both sprinted desperately back for the rocks, but Bradbury never made it. Private Mark James was shot in the back and wrist, but he managed to crawl toward the rocks until his teammates grabbed him and pulled him to cover.

Behind the rocks, Sergeants Monti, Cunningham, and Hawes returned fire to give their teammates cover. In front of the rocks, Sergeant Patrick Lybert lay behind a small stone wall, using controlled bursts from his M4 to suppress the enemy fire and give his teammates a chance. In a matter of minutes, the patrol was badly bloodied and pinned down.

At that desperate hour, Staff Sergeants Jared Monti and Christopher Cunningham took charge of the defense. They posted soldiers in a ragged perimeter around the rocks to protect their flanks and directed return fire. Monti grabbed the radio handset, cleared the network, and calmly informed headquarters of the dire situation: His patrol was under attack, badly outnumbered by an estimated fifty enemy fighters, and in immediate danger of being overrun and killed. Hawes fired his grenade launcher at the approaching insurgents to give Monti a moment's cover to look over the rock and assess the enemy's position. Then they ducked back down as machine-gun bullets ricocheted above their heads in answer. Monti relayed accurate grid coordinates for the enemy's location, calling in fires "danger close."

The insurgents were so close that the men could easily hear the Afghans barking orders. With two machine guns on the mountainside above keeping the Americans pinned down, the Afghan fighters split into two groups to flank the patrol on either side of their position. In the intense firefight, members of the patrol saw Sergeant Lybert's head slump forward and blood pour out of his ears. The fire was too heavy for a medic to reach him, but Specialist Daniel Linnihan crawled toward the stone wall and was able to grab Lybert's weapon and drag it back behind the rocks.

In danger of being outflanked, Monti dropped the radio

handset and fired staccato bursts from his M4 at a group of fighters closing on their western flank. The enemy approached to within just ten meters of their position, and Monti threw a grenade at their feet. It was a dud, but the Afghan fighters scattered for cover, buying the patrol precious seconds. Monti then went back to the radio and continued to relay coordinates for supporting fire.

Moments later a volley of mortar rounds fell in the midst of the Afghan fighters with earth-shaking explosions, killing some and driving the rest back to the tree line. Sergeants Monti and Cunningham took the brief respite to try and account for all their soldiers. They quickly realized that Private First Class Brian Bradbury, a machine gunner in Monti's team, was unaccounted for. Jared Monti shouted his name again and again. Finally, over the din of battle they heard Bradbury's weak voice telling them that he was badly injured and unable to move. He lay in a shallow depression not twenty yards in front of the rock formation his teammates were using as cover. The depression prevented them from seeing Bradbury, but it also kept him out of view of the Afghan insurgents just thirty yards beyond. Out in the open, Bradbury was exposed not only to enemy fire, but to incoming U.S. mortar rounds.

They knew Bradbury was hit and badly injured, but the young soldier wasn't screaming or even moaning. He stayed quiet unless they shouted a question, and then he would answer as calm as can be. He was some kind of soldier, all right.

"You'll be all right, Bradbury! We're coming to get you!" Jared Monti shouted.

"I'll go and get him, Monti!" Staff Sergeant Cunningham shouted across the rocks.

"No, Bradbury's my soldier," Monti shouted back. "I'm going for him!"

Everyone still left alive in the patrol understood the odds Jared Monti was up against, and the wall of hellfire that awaited him just on the other side of the rocks. They couldn't even pop their head above the rocks to aim a rifle without risking getting it shot off. No one knew the odds better than Monti himself. But Bradbury was out there wounded and exposed, and he had to try and bring his soldier back. None of Monti's teammates even questioned the decision; they just prepared to give him cover.

"Here, take this," Staff Sergeant Monti said to Sergeant Christopher Grzecki as he handed over the radio handset and his own call sign. "You are now Chaos Three-Five."

Monti tightened the chinstrap on his Kevlar helmet and then he was gone, moving from the protection of the large rocks, running low and fast as fire from the nearby tree line and enemy machine guns erupted in an awful din. He made it to within a few yards of Bradbury, but the impact geysers spewing all around his feet were thick as a rain squall, and he was forced to sprint back and dive behind the low stone wall where Sergeant Lybert lay. Monti paused for a moment to catch his breath, and he verified that his friend was indeed dead. He called for covering fire again, and once again Jared Monti broke from cover and ran in the direction of Bradbury before intense enemy fire forced him to dive back behind the wall.

From behind the rock Sergeant Hawes shouted that he was down to his last 40mm grenade. The desperate odds of trying to save Private Bradbury were now clear to everyone. But Jared Monti was committed to getting his soldier out, damn the odds.

"I've gotta get him," Monti shouted. "I'm going again!"

On the count, Sergeant Hawes fired his last 40mm grenade at the closest Afghan position in the tree line and Monti broke from cover and sprinted directly for Bradbury at a full run. The patrol fired every weapon, trying desperately to suppress the enemy incoming. Hawes fired his M4 in controlled bursts until he ran out of ammo, dropping behind the rock to change out magazines. At that moment a rocket-propelled grenade whizzed into the clearing and exploded nearly at Jared Monti's feet.

"I'm hit!" Monti screamed, trying to crawl back toward the stone wall, but too badly torn up to make it.

By then it was almost dark, and U.S. artillery and mortar rounds were finding their mark, pounding the enemy positions and driving the insurgents back. Close air support aircraft had also come on station, dropping heavy bombs to further dislodge the Afghans from the mountainside.

From behind the rocks, soldiers called out to Jared Monti, encouraging him to stay awake. Monti told them that it was all right, he had made his peace with God. Then he asked Staff Sergeant Christopher Cunningham to tell his parents that he loved them. After that he fell silent. It was pitch dark by the time they reached Private Bradbury. He was still alive and able to talk, but Brian Bradbury would not survive the night on that desolate ridge.

The next morning the patrol found several blood trails near the enemy positions, but no bodies. A medivac helicopter picked up the bodies of Private First Class Brian Bradbury, Sergeant Patrick Lybert, and Staff Sergeant Jared Monti. The rest of the ill-fated patrol moved off on foot, making their way off the mountain with heavy hearts and the realization that they had witnessed the rarest kind of valor.

For Staff Sergeant Cunningham, watching Jared Monti brave death two times to try and reach his fallen comrade, only to be repelled, and then to face nearly certain death yet again in his determination, was simply the bravest thing he had ever seen a soldier do. His selfless actions exemplified the "above and beyond the call of duty" highlighted in Monti's Medal of Honor citation.

"I've lost lots and lots of friends in the military," Sergeant John Hawes would later recall about Jared Monti's heroism. "There's nothing glorious about dying or death, but there is nothing greater than dying for something you believe in—dying trying to help somebody. That just puts so much meaning into your death, and into your life. That's worth dying for."

Chapter 7

———☆———

Saint Michael's Day

Navy Petty Officer (SEAL)
Michael A. Monsoor

The streets of Malaab were strewn with trash and rubble and the burned-out husks of cars, and many of the ochre-colored buildings were pockmarked by bullet impacts. The vibe was one of hidden menace. In 2006, Malaab was the most violent district in the most dangerous city in all of war-torn Iraq. Graffiti spray-painted on the walls in Ramadi reflected the confidence of the Al Qaeda terrorists and Sunni insurgents who had made the city their stronghold, reading simply "The graveyard of the Americans."

A cloud of dust rose over a convoy of Iraqi Army vehicles as they completed a counterinsurgency sweep. A platoon of Navy SEAL commandos conducting overwatch for the operation were preparing to withdraw when the familiar rattle of automatic weapons fire sounded. Immediately one of the SEALs crumpled to the ground with a leg wound. Another day, another fight to the death in the battle for Ramadi.

In an instant two SEAL commandos broke from cover and sprinted to their wounded teammate, bullets screeching all around. Together they dragged their teammate to safety as one of the SEAL commandos kept firing his Mk 48 machine gun with his other arm, laying down suppressive fire. As his wounded teammate was treated behind cover, the machine gunner kept up his furious rate of fire, the metallic punch of the big weapon echoing off the nearby walls. Only when an armored Humvee wheeled up did the machine gunner break contact, just long enough to help load his wounded teammate for evacuation.

Petty Officer Michael Monsoor would receive the Silver Star for valor for his actions on that day in May 2006, but no one in Delta Platoon, Naval Special Warfare Task Group–Arabian Peninsula was surprised by his audacity or cool head under fire. The SEAL commandos of Task Unit Bruiser (TUB) had been in violent contact with the enemy virtually from the moment they touched down in Malaab, and Monsoor always seemed to be in the thick of it, walking point and shielding his teammates with suppressive fire during frequent firefights. Even in what would become the most highly decorated SEAL team since Vietnam, it was like they all said: "Mikey" Monsoor, with his crooked grin and Southern California cool, was something special.

Growing up in Garden Grove, California, Monsoor seemed an unlikely prospect for elite warrior status. As a young child his asthma was so bad that it sent him to the hospital on more than one occasion. But he would still challenge his three siblings and friends to races in the swimming pool, and over time he developed into an excellent athlete. By high school he began filling out his six-foot-one, 210-pound frame, and he played tight end on the Argonauts football team for Garden Grove High School. By graduation, he was a good-looking Southern California teenager with a mischievous grin and a shock of dark hair. He loved spearfishing, snowboarding, and driving his Corvette sports car.

But there was much more to Michael Monsoor than just California cool. His father, George, was a former Marine, and his mother, Sally, a social worker. Older brother James was a former Marine and a police officer. Sister Sara was a nurse. His younger brother, Joseph, was a college football player. Service and helping others were part of the Monsoor family values, an attitude informed by a deep Catholic faith. So when Monsoor enlisted in the Navy in 2001, and survived grueling BUD/S training to become an elite SEAL commando in 2004, there was pride but not a lot of surprise that Michael Monsoor had volunteered to walk point in America's post-9/11 wars. And by 2006, the Iraq front in that struggle teetered on a razor's edge.

Through its wanton slaughter of Shiite Muslim civilians, the Sunni terrorist group Al Qaeda in Iraq (AQI) was very close to succeeding with its strategy of igniting an all-out sectarian civil war that would drive U.S. forces from the country in defeat. In June 2006, U.S. Special Forces would kill the "emir" of AQI, the brutish Jordanian Abu Musab al-Zarqawi, who had the blood of thousands on his hands. But AQI's fanatical fighters and suicide bombers continued their relentless campaign of mass murder from the group's base of operations in a string of hardscrabble towns along the Euphrates River in Iraq's Anbar Province. Their names are etched in the annals of urban warfare, synonymous with some of the most brutal fighting in the long Iraq War: Fallujah. Haditha. Hit. Ramadi.

No area of the dusty riverside city of Ramadi was more hotly contested than the Malaab district, where SEAL Team 3, Task Unit Ramadi operated. By September 2006, near the end of its six-month deployment, the SEAL task force had already fought in thirty-five separate firefights, killing scores of enemy fighters and capturing many more. Whether it was hunting Al Qaeda mortar teams along the banks of the Euphrates River or patrolling the streets of Malaab that "seemed paved with fire," in the words of one SEAL commando, Task Unit Ramadi came under enemy attack on an overwhelming majority of its missions. By the fall U.S. forces were suffering an average of thirty troops killed in action each month in Anbar Province, and many more wounded.

Yet the U.S. troops pushed on, and their sacrifices and determination made a difference. Working with Army and Marine Corps infantry and Iraqi Army units, SEAL Team 3 was helping to pacify the most violent city in Anbar, convincing local Sunni tribal sheiks that U.S. forces were in the fight for the duration. Fed up with the murderous ways and dictates of the Islamist extremists of Al Qaeda in Iraq, a group of Sunni sheiks were banding together to form the Anbar Salvation Council, finding common cause with U.S. forces and increasingly committing their tribesmen to the fight against the terrorist group. Their movement would become the storied "Anbar Awakening," and with the backing of U.S. forces it would deal a decisive defeat to Al Qaeda in Iraq. Yet that progress came at a steep price.

September 29 is Saint Michael's Day, venerated for the warrior saint who appears when dangers gather close, and its dawning in 2006 found the SEALs of Task Unit Ramadi on their final mission in Iraq. After months of humping and fighting in the streets of the city, frequently in scorching heat that soared past 120 degrees, the SEAL commandos were burned out. They'd had their fill of the constant danger that accompanied every trip outside the wire, and they missed their families and ached for the homecoming that was just a week away. Yet they still had one last mission to accomplish.

Operation Kentucky Jumper was a battalion clearance mission in southern Ramadi. Machine gunner Michael Monsoor and three fellow SEALs, along with four Iraqi Army soldiers, manned a sniper overwatch position on a rooftop in a residential neighborhood, guarding the western flank of the main operation. Shortly after dawn they saw four insurgents armed with AK-47 automatic rifles slipping among the houses on an obvious reconnaissance mission. The SEAL snipers fired, killing one of the enemy fighters and wounding another.

After they had given away their position with the contact, word soon came over the radio that local civilians were blocking off the roads into the area and warning other people away.

Soon a loudspeaker began blasting from a nearby mosque, and the Iraqi soldiers confirmed that it was a warning to insurgents of the presence of the SEAL snipers, and a call to arms. Within the hour the sniper team exchanged fire with insurgents in a passing vehicle, and their building was hit with a rocket-propelled grenade. Still, the SEALs held their ground to keep the operation's flank from collapsing.

Michael Monsoor repositioned his heavy machine gun in the direction of the enemy's most likely approach. He was on a small outcropping on the roof ringed by a low wall, keeping guard over two SEAL snipers as they lay prone on the roof and peered through their rifle scopes. Monsoor looked over the wall through a tactical periscope, searching for enemy movement.

Something hit Monsoor on the chest, bouncing off his body armor and falling at his feet. He leapt to his feet and yelled "Grenade!" but immediately saw that while he could reach cover, his teammates had no chance of escaping the blast. Without hesitation, he threw himself on the grenade, smothering it and absorbing the full blast to save his teammates. He died of his wounds a short time later.

One of the survivors spared by Monsoor's heroism spoke of him as a guardian angel. "Mikey looked death in the face that day and said, 'You cannot take my brothers. I will go in their stead.'"

Chief Warrant Officer Benjamin Oleson was on the rooftop that day next to Monsoor. "All I heard was 'Grenade!' and the next thing I know was the explosion," he said. "All I can say is that I'm alive today because of what Mikey did, because of him going down on that grenade. I now have a family and three kids, and I owe all of that to Mikey. So, the moments I had with Mikey I cherish every day. I talk about him a lot with my kids, so that they understand."

When they buried Michael Monsoor at Fort Rosecrans National Cemetery near San Diego, many of the SEALs on the West Coast lined up in a long procession and as they filed past removed the golden tridents from their uniforms and pressed them onto the top of the wooden casket. Witnesses said the sound they made pounding the badges into the casket echoed across the whole cemetery that day.

"The procession went on nearly half an hour," President George W. Bush said at the April 8, 2008, ceremony presenting parents George and Sally Monsoor with their son's posthumous Medal of Honor. "And when it was all over, the simple wooden coffin had become a gold-plated memorial to a hero who will never be forgotten." The U.S. Navy would later honor those words, commissioning its newest destroyer the USS *Michael Monsoor*.

Chapter 8

————☆————

The Hardest Choice

Army Private First Class Ross A. McGinnis

om McGinnis was at his home in the small town of Knox, Pennsylvania, when he received an email from his son. Ross was only nineteen years old, and half a world away in Schweinfurt, Germany, deployed as a soldier in the U.S. Army's 26th Infantry Regiment. He sounded a little down and probably homesick, with too much time on his hands. In the email, Ross McGinnis apologized for all the trouble he had caused his parents in high school, and Tom had to admit his boy had been a handful.

There had been police at the door a couple of times. When he was barely a teenager Ross had been expelled from school for a time for buying pot on campus and having a couple of knives in his locker. Then there was the time when he was on probation that he got caught for hiding a stolen bicycle for a friend. Even after being readmitted to Clarion County High School, he continued to struggle mightily to maintain even passing grades. Ross just didn't seem to have it in him to buckle down at school.

And yet he was a good athlete, loyal to a fault as a friend, and one of the funniest kids you'd ever want to meet. One of his fellow soldiers said Ross was the only recruit in boot camp who could make even the drill instructors laugh, and that was saying something. His wisecracking sense of humor and love of mischief reminded his father of the cartoon character Bart Simpson.

And yet when it came to soldiering, young Ross McGinnis was suddenly all about getting it right. He had dreamed of
being a soldier since kindergarten and took to the profession
immediately. At six feet tall and probably 160 pounds soaking wet, McGinnis was probably the skinniest soldier in the
outfit, but he manned the big .50 caliber machine gun and
never shirked a difficult task. His frequent hijinks and infectious can-do spirit also kept his teammates loose, which is
how commanders want their troops in the field.

All of which explained why Tom McGinnis was somewhat
surprised at his son's somber email making apologies from Germany. The truth was that Tom might have apologized himself
for not being a better father. But you don't get to go back in
this life, you have to move forward, and Ross was doing that.
In Tom McGinnis's eyes, his son was a hero for standing up
for his country and volunteering to soldier in a time of war. So
McGinnis wrote an email telling his son that there was nothing
in the world Ross could do to keep his father from loving him.

Soon after, the telephone rang in their home in Knox.

"You son of a bitch!" Ross McGinnis told his father. "You
made me cry!"

Sergeant First Class Cedric Thomas had just arrived in the 26th
Infantry Regiment when a tall, lanky soldier came out of the
arms room and extended his hand. As he shook the sergeant's
hand vigorously, Specialist Ross McGinnis introduced himself

with a mischievous grin, and then started laughing. Sergeant Thomas looked down to see his hand covered in black carbon soot from McGinnis's .50 caliber machine gun that the young soldier had been cleaning. The humor was a good sign, and once Sergeant Thomas saw that McGinnis could knock the targets down with the big gun during live-fire training, he knew McGinnis was his gunner.

In August 2006, the 26th Regiment deployed to Baghdad's hardscrabble Adhamiyah district, an overwhelmingly Sunni neighborhood and a stronghold of the resistance to the U.S. presence. The capital was already on the verge of an all-out sectarian civil war between Sunni insurgents and Shiite death squads, whose handiwork was revealed each morning in the dead bodies that littered alleyways and vacant lots. The undisguised hostility of the local populace quickly began to wear on the U.S. soldiers as they patrolled the dusty streets of the neighborhood.

The Abu Hanifa Mosque that dominated the main square of Adhamiyah was the site of former Iraqi dictator Saddam Hussein's final speech before the U.S. invasion in 2003. In the speech, Saddam exhorted his countrymen to "defend themselves, their homes, their wives, their children, and their holy shrines," and he promised to fight alongside them "in the same trenches." Then Saddam retreated behind the gates of one of his many Baghdad palaces.

Adhamiyah was the birthplace of Saddam's fascist Baath Party, and it remained a bastion of hardcore support for the former dictator. U.S. and Iraqi government troops frequently had to seal off the neighborhood to avoid ambushes and quell raging gun battles on the streets. The fact that Saddam Hussein had been captured, sentenced to death, and would soon be hanged only added to the atmosphere of menace and resentment that permeated Adhamiyah.

After completing its third patrol of the day, C Company's 1st Platoon returned to the unit's heavily fortified forward operating base in Adhamiyah just before sunset on December 4, 2006. As they drove their armored Humvees past the tactical operations center, the company commander came out.

"Hey, you guys are finished with your last patrol, so I need you to go out again and see to a faulty generator at these coordinates," he said.

"Roger that, sir," said Sergeant First Class Cedric Thomas, who organized his platoon back into a six-vehicle convoy. Within minutes, they were rolling out the gates again into the mean streets of Adhamiyah. Sergeant Thomas was in the critical "six o'clock" position at the end of the convoy, protecting its rear with the rest of his Humvee crew: Staff Sergeant Ian Newland, Sergeant Lyle Buehler, and Specialists Sean Lawson and Ross McGinnis, who, as always, stood in the turret and manned the big .50 caliber machine gun.

Roughly a thousand meters past the gate the convoy turned into a neighborhood of two- and three-story buildings on either side of the street. As the last Humvee made the turn, McGinnis swiveled the machine gun toward a rooftop and then seemed to bat at something with an "Oh shit!" They heard something clang off the radio mount inside the Humvee even as McGinnis shouted over the headset.

"Grenade! It's in the truck!"

In the split seconds between the reaction and the explosion the strapped-in crew instinctively clenched into a protective crouch, averting their faces from the deadly blast. McGinnis had the only escape route through the top of the machine gun turret, but instead of jumping out he dropped down into the Humvee and trapped the grenade between the armored bulkhead and his back, smothering it with his own body to give his team members a chance at life.

The detonation blew open the heavy armored doors of the Humvee. In the smoke and confusion, Sergeant Thomas found himself outside the vehicle engaging the ambushers on the rooftops and in doorways with his M4 rifle. The rest of the patrol vehicles circled back and formed a defensive perimeter as they loaded the casualties and sped off to the first aid station. Nineteen-year-old Ross Andrew McGinnis died of the terrible wounds he absorbed in order to save the lives of his four friends.

After the funeral his parents were going through all of the photographs of their son. There was Ross as a youngster in the Boy Scouts, playing basketball and soccer at the YMCA, mountain biking and playing video games as a teenager. And then there was Ross as a soldier, outfitted in his "battle rattle" and giving an "all's good" signal from his machine-gun turret, brandishing his M4 rifle, posing with his arms slung around his fellow soldiers. In those photographs Ross is always grinning into the camera like a man elated to discover exactly what he was meant to do in life, and who he was meant to do it with.

"We never realized until after he was killed, and we pulled out all these pictures, and in all of his pictures in the Army his smile is just fluorescent!" his mother, Romayne McGinnis, said, speaking in an episode of *Wired Outdoors*. "Whether he was in Germany or Iraq, Ross just had a big smile on his face that definitely wasn't there in high school."

The recognition that Ross McGinnis died doing what he loved brought some consolation to his parents, as did the posthumous Medal of Honor received from President George W. Bush on June 2, 2008. Today the Veterans of Foreign Wars Post 2145 in Clarion, Pennsylvania, is named after their son, and the residents of Knox created a memorial bench at the local high school in his honor. And over time the overwhelming sense of grief his parents felt was surpassed by pride that when suddenly confronted with the hardest choice of all—between survival and self-sacrifice on behalf of his four Army brothers—Ross McGinnis chose honorably.

"Everyone is going to die, but it's how you die that really makes a difference," Tom McGinnis told Staff Sergeant Ian Newland, one of the soldiers saved by his son's heroism, on *Wired Outdoors*. "So Ross died well. And I could not be more proud of him."

Chapter 9

—☆—

A Soldier's Calling

Army Staff Sergeant Travis W. Atkins

Jack and Elaine Atkins enjoyed having their son back safe in Bozeman, the scenic valley town in southwestern Montana where he had grown into an avid outdoorsman. In the summer, Travis still liked to hunt and fish in the thick forests of the Rockies, and in the winter he rode snowmobiles on the snow-blanketed mountainsides.

After serving a tour in Iraq with the 101st Airborne in 2003, Travis had left the U.S. Army behind and pretty much picked up where he left off after high school. He worked as a contractor pouring concrete and painting houses and took a few classes at the University of Montana in Missoula. Yet there was a restlessness in Travis Atkins that was not unusual for a former soldier back from war.

Jack Atkins had served as a paratrooper in the Vietnam War, so he understood the difficulty of adjusting back to civilian life. Travis had been fascinated by the military since he was a young boy, and he had taken to it naturally. Back in 2001 his parents had traveled all the way from Bozeman to Fort Benning, Georgia, to celebrate their son's graduation from basic training. A lot of his fellow recruits grumbled about the deprivations of boot camp and the verbal abuse of drill sergeants, but not their son. Travis told his parents that meeting the challenges of basic training was the most fun he ever experienced in his life.

Travis had served as an infantryman and fire team leader

in the 101st Airborne Division during the invasion of Iraq in 2003. Under the leadership of division commander Major General David Petraeus, one of the most heralded leaders of his generation of officers, the 101st "Screaming Eagles" had seen combat the length of Iraq during the invasion, crossing into southern Iraq at the Kuwaiti border and fighting all the way to the northern city of Mosul.

After ten months in Iraq, Travis Atkins planned on reenlisting. Yet, ever the outdoorsman, he had his heart set on serving in the 501st Infantry Regiment in Alaska. When the Army personnel office couldn't make it happen, Travis was out of there. He returned to civilian life in Bozeman instead and didn't seem to look back.

Only sometimes it's easier to take the man out of the Army than to take the army out of the man. By the end of 2005, the U.S. Army was losing the fight to stabilize Iraq as the country was coming apart along its sectarian seams between Sunnis and Shiites. Travis Atkins was restless. His parents really weren't surprised when he told them, nearly two years to the month after receiving an honorable discharge, that he was reenlisting in the U.S. Army. Travis, who was then thirty years old, knew he was a better noncommissioned officer than most, and he loved leading young troops in the field. He also knew that the U.S. Army desperately needed all hands on the rifle stock.

When he re-upped and was assigned to the 10th Mountain Division, Travis and his family understood that he would soon return to war. In August 2006, Jack and Elaine Atkins thus traveled across the country once again, this time to witness the 2nd Brigade Combat Team's deployment ceremony at Fort Drum, New York. As they sat in the reviewing stands and watched their son and his fellow soldiers march across the field in tight formations with flags flying, they knew with a terrible certainty that some of those proud young men and women on the field that day would not be coming back home.

Yet the Atkinses didn't question their son's decision to reenlist. As those who knew him best could tell you, when Travis Atkins joined the U.S. Army he found his calling.

"Travis knew the reality of serving in Iraq. He knew the danger," Jack Atkins would later recall. "But the civilian life just didn't do it for him. He had to get back to the Army."

Iraq in 2006–7 was among the worst places on earth, and the area south of Baghdad that U.S. troops nicknamed the "Triangle of Death" was one of the most hostile and violent in the entire country. A largely agricultural area of orchards and fields and dusty farming towns, it was intersected by the Euphrates River and crisscrossed by deep irrigation canals. The Triangle was also a stronghold for Al Qaeda in Iraq and its fanatical fighters, who used it as a staging area for suicide bombing attacks in Baghdad. They regularly seeded the local dirt roads and intersections along the canals with roadside bombs.

In the summer of 2006 when Staff Sergeant Travis Atkins's

2nd Battalion, 14th Infantry Regiment arrived in the triangle, AQI fighters ambushed and captured two U.S. soldiers near Yusufiyah, later torturing and beheading them and using their remains to draw the search team into a web of improvised explosive devices. The year before, an AQI suicide bomber detonated his explosive belt in a crowded marketplace in the town of Musayyib, igniting a nearby fuel truck and incinerating nearly one hundred Iraqi civilians in one of the worst mass murders of the long Iraq War. Such was a tour of duty in the Triangle of Death.

Late in the morning on June 1, 2007, Staff Sergeant Atkins and his fifteen-soldier squad were manning an observation post on Route Caprice, a dirt road leading through the small town of Abu Samak. The temperature was already heading north of 100 degrees, but nothing seemed out of the ordinary in the quiet streets. Then again, in the Triangle, that could always change in a flash.

In their nearly yearlong tour in Iraq, Atkins and his armored Humvee crew had already survived four teeth-rattling roadside bombs. Though he was sometimes a tough taskmaster, Atkins had repeatedly proven himself cool and unflappable under fire, earning the respect and affection of his soldiers.

The radio in the Humvee crackled with the news from another outlook that four "military-aged men" were advancing through the town, acting suspiciously. Atkins instructed his driver, Private First Class Michael Kistel, to drive to the next intersection. They immediately spotted two of the young men, who looked to be no more than teenagers. Sergeant Atkins opened his heavily armored door, left his M4 rifle next to his seat in the Humvee, and approached the Iraqis with his arms spread wide in a universal gesture of friendliness.

"You look upset," Atkins joked as he approached the young men to question them. "Let me give you a hug."

Before the U.S. soldiers knew what had happened, the search had gone all wrong. Atkins was suddenly wrestling violently with one of the young Iraqis, trying to pin his arms as the man reached for something under his clothes. At that moment of fatal realization, Atkins wrapped the insurgent in a bear hug and threw him to the ground away from his soldiers, and then smothered the man's body with his own to shield his nearby troops. They disappeared in the deafening explosion of the suicide vest.

Atkins's medic had exited the rear of the Humvee and trained his rifle on the other insurgent at the first sign of struggle. Before the dust settled the second Iraqi charged the truck and the medic opened fire, hitting him multiple times. The Iraqi collapsed near the driver's-side door just as Kistel was shutting it, and the explosion from the second suicide vest rocked the Humvee, ending with a thud as the suicide bomber's severed leg landed on the hood of the truck.

Days before he sacrificed his own life to save his soldiers, Staff Sergeant Travis Atkins had called his son, Trevor, to wish him a happy eleventh birthday. Travis was open with his young son about why he had to be away in a dangerous place, as soldiers must: Travis told young Trevor he had a job to do, and there were some very bad men who didn't like Americans very much, and they had to be dealt with.

Twelve years later, Trevor Atkins visited the White House to accept his father's posthumous Medal of Honor. Before the ceremony, he met with many of his father's fellow soldiers from the 10th Mountain Division, who regaled him with funny and poignant stories of the man and soldier who was his father.

"The Medal of Honor means the world to me. I can't thank everyone enough for the support and everything they've done to give him that, because he truly deserves it," Trevor would later say. "But my true treasure is what people say about him. That's what makes me most proud. He was a great soldier and a great father."

Chapter 10

——✫——

Rock Avalanche

Army Specialist Salvatore A. Giunta

The CH-47 Chinook transports flew up a narrow valley barely a kilometer across at its widest point, the machine gunners in the open rear doors staring out at a mountainous landscape of stark beauty and isolation. The big helicopters settled in a cloud of dust and the "Sky Soldiers" of Battle Company, 2nd Battalion of the 503rd Infantry Regiment, 173rd Airborne Brigade, filed out onto the patch of fortified rock and dirt they would defend for most of the next fifteen months: Combat Outpost Korengal.

The Korengal Valley is a deep gash roughly six miles long carved out of the mountains of northeastern Afghanistan by a tributary of the Pech River. The valley provided a natural infiltration route for Taliban and Al Qaeda fighters flowing from the wild tribal areas of nearby Pakistan toward the Afghan capital of Kabul, where they launched bloody attacks on Afghan security forces and soft civilian targets alike, and frequently detonated suicide bombs, causing mass casualties, in a campaign to destabilize the government. The mission of the 173rd Airborne was to try and win the trust of local tribal leaders and impede that flow of guerrilla fighters and terrorists.

In May 2007, Battle Company had a reputation as a gung-ho outfit. Many of the soldiers were combat veterans with earlier deployments to Afghanistan and Iraq. You gave them a mission and Battle Company tended to get on it without a lot of questions. Yet even before they fully unloaded their kit, there were signs that time in the Korengal was not going to be like other combat deployments. The soldiers in the unit that Battle Company was replacing stayed huddled off to themselves, not even bothering to greet the newcomers or shake hands. Some of them were talking to themselves as they loaded up their gear to leave.

"They wanted nothing to do with us, and none of us understood why," Staff Sergeant Erick Gallardo, a Battle Company squad leader, later told a reporter from *60 Minutes*. "It wasn't long afterward that we figured out why they didn't want to talk to us. That valley just took every ounce of life out of you."

For U.S. troops, life in the Korengal meant waking up every day burdened by a sense of unrelenting malice. The ridgelines and craggy ravines rippling to the horizon like waves offered infinite cover for the countless enemy fighters in the valley who were intent on murder. After a time, the mountains themselves seemed a malign presence, their treacherous heights conspiring against foreign intruders, even the Sky Soldiers of the 173rd Airborne. The Taliban routinely ambushed the U.S. soldiers on patrol. They hit isolated outposts so frequently with rockets and sniper fire that some troops refused to risk the short walk to the crapper. They would huddle behind barriers and hold it in all day, only daring to relieve themselves at night.

Private First Class Juan "Doc" Restrepo was one of the first

Battle Company soldiers to fall in the Korengal. A beloved medic, Restrepo was a twenty-year-old naturalized American citizen by way of Colombia, the kind of soldier who was quick to take the shift of a sick comrade or try and cheer up a homesick buddy. On July 22, 2007, his patrol was ambushed, and during the firefight Restrepo lifted his head above cover to see if any of his fellow soldiers were wounded and needed help. He took bullets to his face and throat. Doc Restrepo's fellow soldiers scrambled to save him, but he died soon after in a medivac helicopter.

Two months later the "Spartans" of 2nd Platoon filed out of Firebase Phoenix in the dead of night and climbed nearly a thousand feet up the mountainside to a spot near where Restrepo fell, and they planted their flag in an act of sheer defiance. Using tarps, plywood, portable generators, and stacked bags full of rocks, they built a small fort in the middle of enemy territory and dared the Taliban to try and kick them off the mountain. The Taliban obliged with almost daily attacks, but the American soldiers fought them off and defended one of the most exposed U.S. outposts in all of Afghanistan like their honor depended on it. The message they intended to send with Outpost Restrepo was clear.

"When the boys built that base the Taliban in the valley were completely in shock," Captain Dan Kearney, Battle Company commander, explained in the award-winning documentary film *Restrepo*. "It was like a middle finger sticking up. When they realized they couldn't knock off OP Restrepo, we had the upper hand."

$\star\ \star\ \star$

In late October 2007, Battle Company launched Operation Rock Avalanche as a final sweep to clear Taliban out of the high mountain villages before winter set in and the fighting season ended. They knew the insurgents would be gunning for them. From their perch high on the mountainside at OP Restrepo they could clearly see enemy fighters carrying weapons and supplies through the villages in the valley below. By the second day of the operation the Taliban were so close that U.S. signals intelligence operators could hear them whispering over their radios so as not to give away their positions to the nearby Americans. The insurgents had never whispered on their radios before.

On October 23, 2007, Battle Company was spread out along a thick forest of spruce trees high up on a mountainside dubbed 2435, conducting overwatch as Chosen Company cleared a village down below. Suddenly they began taking heavy fire from a nearby ridgeline, which pinned many of the soldiers down. At the top of the hillside, Staff Sergeant Larry Rougle had characteristically taken a position in the middle of the American line to guard the formation. Before his fellow soldiers could reach him, Rougle's position was overrun, and he was killed with a shot to the forehead. Sergeant Kevin Rice and Specialist Carl Vandenberge were also shot and badly wounded.

A legendary paratrooper in the 173rd, Staff Sergeant

Rougle was on his sixth combat deployment. He had seemed invincible to his fellow troops, but that kind of devotion to duty rarely went untested in the Korengal. His loss hit the entire battalion hard.

"He was one of the best, if not the best," said Sergeant Rice, who was wounded in the attack, speaking to the filmmakers. "I think that's what was tough for a lot of people, was kind of knowing in the back of your mind, 'Well, if the best guy we have out here just got killed, where's that put me? What's going to happen to me, you know? What's going to happen to the guys on my left and my right?' "

Because the Taliban fighters had captured weapons and gear from Sergeant Rougle and some of the wounded in action, including a sniper rifle and two sets of night-vision goggles, Captain Kearney decided to send his troops to try and retrieve the equipment. They had plenty of airpower as backup, including two Apache helicopter gunships, two armed Predator drones, and a B-1 bomber on call. "As the commander on the ground I made the decision that we would go down into Landigal and get our damn weapons back and show these guys we weren't going to give up," he said. "Because we don't leave anything behind. I don't want them to have a 'war trophy.' I don't want them walking around showing off Sergeant Rice's M14 [sniper rifle], or Sergeant Rougle's backpack. Hell no, that stuff is ours."

As Battle Company's platoons moved into position above Landigal, signals intelligence operators reported a new message coming over the enemy's radio net. The Taliban fighters were saying that in the battle to come the trophy they most wanted was the body of an American soldier.

As Sergeant Rougle's position was being attacked two days earlier, twenty-two-year-old Specialist Salvatore Giunta had sat in his fighting position listening to the radio and the far-off echo of the firefight, wishing he could do something. There were frantic calls that an American position was getting overrun, that there were wounded in action, that someone was not answering their radio. There were calls for a medivac helicopter. Giunta could only sit there tight-lipped, marinating in his anger and pissed off that he couldn't do anything but pray the situation was not as bad as it sounded. But this being the Korengal it was probably worse.

Only a few years earlier Giunta had been leading a typical teenager's life in the small town of Florence, Iowa, population a few thousand, going to high school and working as a "sandwich artist" in a Subway shop. Then the 9/11 terrorist attacks happened, the country was suddenly at war in Afghanistan and Iraq, and Sal Giunta was a young, able-bodied American male. So he joined the U.S. Army.

By October 2007, Giunta was already on his second combat deployment to Afghanistan. He remembered the excitement and enthusiasm of that first deployment, when he and the other newbies were throwing off sparks, armed to the teeth and going to war! The loss of close friends and comrades had mostly bled away the excitement, but when a nineteen-year-old Giunta returned home and contemplated getting out, an Army stretched thin by a two-front war issued a "stop loss" order freezing all separations.

When he was deployed back to Afghanistan, Giunta recalled the advice his team leader had given him on that first deployment: "You just got to try to do everything you can, when it's your time to do it."

On October 25, 2007, Sal Giunta and the rest of 1st Platoon had remained high on a mountain ridge known as the Gatigal Spur, providing overwatch for 2nd and 3rd Platoons as they searched unsuccessfully for the missing U.S. weaponry in Landigal village. Once the search was completed, 1st Platoon was the last unit to head back to base at the conclusion of Operation Rock Avalanche.

By nightfall the soldiers were beyond exhaustion after tense days of hiking and repositioning, and they trudged single file along the crest of a ridgeline. A nearly full moon bathed the mountainside in a pale light so bright the soldiers didn't even bother with their night-vision goggles, and they carefully walked a path that dropped off steeply into shadowy forest on both sides of the spur.

Specialist Giunta was fourth in line when the volcano erupted. A shower of tracer fire that seemed to him as thick as stars in the night sky engulfed the formation. Rocket-propelled grenades screamed in and burst in their midst, the fireballs illuminating the trees at crazy angles. The roar of machine guns and automatic weapons fired at point-blank range came from multiple directions, the whiz and snap of bullets crackling all around.

Walking point at the front of the patrol, Sergeant Joshua Brennan and Specialist Frank Eckrode were cut down immediately. Their medic, Specialist Hugo Mendoza, was hit and fell. Just ahead, Specialist Giunta saw Sergeant Gallardo's head snap back at an unnatural angle as he stumbled and fell into a ditch, hit in the helmet by an AK-47 round. Giunta ran forward and pulled Gallardo back toward cover, taking two bullets to his own body armor and equipment that felt like being shoved hard by an unseen hand. Above their heads two Apache gunships circled impotently, unable to fire because of the closeness of the combatants.

First Platoon had stumbled into a classic L-shaped ambush, with a dozen or more insurgents firing from just twenty or thirty feet away into the front and along the left side of their patrol. A military investigation would later determine that the enemy used an inordinate number of tracers and concentrated its rocket and automatic weapons fire to throw up a "wall of lead" designed to separate the lead element from the rest of the unit, the better to overrun and capture them.

But Specialist Sal Giunta and Sergeant Erick Gallardo had other ideas.

In a choreography of battle that was as instinctual as it was desperate, Giunta quickly directed his fire team members to lay down fields of fire so the enemy couldn't roll them up from the rear. Then, using the disorienting impact of fragmentation grenades as cover, Giunta, Gallardo, and SAW gunner Private First Class Kaleb Casey advanced steadily into the face of the enemy fire to find their wounded teammates. Three times they paused to toss more grenades, and Private Garrett Clary gave them additional cover with his M203 grenade launcher.

They reached Specialist Frank Eckrode first. The young soldier had managed to find a bit of cover and return fire until his SAW jammed. By the time Gallardo and Giunta found him, Eckrode had been shot four times, and he was nearly hysterical as they tried to treat his wounds.

"I saw them! They've got him!" Eckrode shouted. "They've got him!"

Before Sergeant Gallardo could make sense of it, Specialist Sal Giunta was up and running into the dark directly toward the enemy position to their front.

Giunta was alone as he burst from the trees that the Taliban ambushers had used for cover and came onto a flat, open area that looked eerie in the blue moonlight. A short way ahead, he clearly saw three men, two of them carrying a third by his arms and legs. At that moment he realized that two Taliban fighters were trying to carry away Sergeant Joshua Brennan, a standout soldier if ever there was one. And then Sal Giunta was running and shooting, running and shooting, desperate to close the gap and reach his best friend.

Giunta shot one of the Taliban through the head and he dropped dead. The other let go of Brennan and started to run. Giunta shot him too. By the time he reached Brennan, Giunta's M4 magazine was empty, and he stopped to tend to his wounded friend. Brennan had been shot all to hell, and he was drifting in and out of consciousness. As he came to and saw Giunta, Brennan asked for morphine and then complained about something in his mouth. Giunta could see that Brennan was missing part of his jaw, but he didn't say anything.

"You'll get out and tell your hero stories and come to visit us in Florence," Giunta assured his friend.

"I will, I will," said Brennan.

Soon Sergeant Gallardo and some of the other soldiers ran up, and for the next half hour they tended to Brennan's many wounds and offered encouragement to their wounded brother until the medivac helicopter arrived and took him away. Then they divided up Brennan's weapons and equipment and started the long, painful walk back to base. Every member of the platoon had been hit at least once by bullets or shrapnel. All the way back Sal Giunta could feel the reassuring weight of Brennan's body armor in his rucksack, and he concentrated on putting one foot in front of the other.

Back at base, Captain Dan Kearney told them that Sergeant Joshua Brennan and Specialist Hugo Mendoza hadn't made it, and 1st Platoon's world came crashing in.

In April 2010, after nearly fifty American soldiers had lost their lives in the Korengal, the U.S. military abandoned the valley for good. With so much bloodshed and loss, most of the soldiers were more than relieved to see the Korengal recede to oblivion out of the rear door of the Chinook helicopter that carried them out of what had become known as "the Valley of Death."

Later that year, Sergeant Salvatore Giunta became the first living soldier since the Vietnam War to receive the Medal of Honor. He was humbled by the honor, but uneasy and resistant to being singled out as exceptional, not when his brothers in arms such as Larry Rougle, Joshua Brennan, and Hugo Mendoza gave their last full measure and sacrificed their lives in the Korengal.

In interviews, Giunta repeatedly insisted that he did only what he was trained to do, and no more than his fellow troops would have done for him in the same situation. *"You just got to try to do everything you can, when it's your time to do it."*

Giunta's fellow soldiers knew the truth. By charging through enemy fire to rescue a fellow soldier, he embodied the warrior ethos of never leaving a fallen comrade behind. His quick reactions and steadiness under fire disrupted a devastating ambush that almost certainly would have claimed many more lives. In recommending him for the Medal of Honor, his commander compared Giunta to Audie Murphy, the most decorated American soldier in World War II, who single-handedly repelled an entire company of German infantry for the same reason that Sal Giunta fought so heroically: "Because they were killing my friends."

No one understood the profound impact of Giunta's bravery more than Sergeant Erick Gallardo, who fought alongside him on the Gatigal Spur, and received a Silver Star for his own heroism that night.

"Giunta saved us from having to go into an even deeper corner of the Korengal Valley where nobody has ever been, and try and find an American soldier," he told *60 Minutes*. "Instead, the last thing Joshua Brennan saw was us. He saw Giunta's face coming up to help. He knew he was home with his family now, because of what Giunta did."

Salvatore Giunta may never be fully at peace with receiving the Medal of Honor, and that's part of the weighty burden of carrying it on behalf of all who answered the call in the Korengal and kept faith with each other.

"This is the nation's highest honor, given to me, but every single person I served with deserves to wear it. They are just as much of me as I am," said Giunta. "So, my name in lights doesn't look that good. But if I can bring everyone else's name with me, then cool. I think that looks good with everyone else's name up there."

Chapter 11

---⭐---

Last Man Standing

Army Specialist Kyle J. White

First Lieutenant Matthew Ferrara and his paratroopers stared in surprise as the men of the village of Aranas continued to file into the crowded room to hold a *shura*, or consultation, council with the Americans. While these were normally small meetings with a handful of village elders, the *shura* on November 9, 2007, was attended by what looked like every village male of fighting age and above. They wanted to know how U.S. troops could make their lives better, and they listened to everything Lieutenant Ferrara had to say through his interpreter. The "Sky Soldiers" of 1st Platoon, Chosen Company, 2nd Battalion of the 503rd Infantry Regiment, 173rd Airborne Brigade started to believe they really could do some good with this outreach.

When the elders of Aranas first invited the U.S. troops to a *shura* council there was a lot of suspicion in the battalion headquarters. Combat Outpost Ranch House, situated on the mountain overlooking the village in the Waygal Valley, had been attacked and nearly overrun months earlier. Eleven U.S. soldiers were wounded, leading to the closure of the outpost. U.S. commanders suspected that the elders of Aranas had colluded in the attack, and ever since there had been little communication with the village.

The night before the meeting, fourteen paratroopers from 1st Platoon and a squad of Afghan National Army soldiers had entered Aranas under the cover of darkness, bunking down in an American-built schoolhouse in the center of the village. The schoolhouse was obviously not being used, an apt metaphor for the well-meaning but often misguided U.S. civil affairs projects designed to win, if not the hearts and minds, at least the grudging cooperation of the local populace.

On the morning of November 9, the scheduled *shura* council was repeatedly pushed back. The Americans were told that morning prayers among the elders had run longer than anticipated. First Platoon was getting antsy by early afternoon, and then seemingly every man in the village showed up to hear what they had to say. Lieutenant Ferrara was encouraged by the big turnout, and detailed other projects besides the schoolhouse that the United States could help launch in the village. Then he was interrupted by Sergeant Phillip Bocks, a Marine Embedded Training Team member. The no-nonsense Bocks said his Afghan interpreter was hearing nearby radio chatter in a language he didn't even recognize. What the hell could that mean?

"Sir, I think it's best that we leave immediately," Bocks told his commander.

Specialist Kyle White was in the middle of the formation as 1st Platoon slowly made its way single file up a series of switchbacks on a steep hillside above the village. Like so many other service members in the all-volunteer force, White had followed the earlier footsteps of his father—Army Special Forces veteran Curt White—into the military. Recent Pentagon data showed that roughly 80 percent of U.S. troops came from a family where at least one parent, grandparent, aunt or uncle, sibling, or cousin had also served in uniform. More than 25 percent of troops have a parent who has served. In that sense, the modern all-volunteer force was something of a family business.

Kyle White was only a freshman in high school back in Bonney Lake, Washington, when the United States was attacked on September 11, 2001. Five years later he was just twenty years old and a low-ranking specialist with twenty-one months in uniform. But time fighting in the Hindu Kush aged you beyond your years.

First Platoon was on a narrow path cut out of the mountainside, a cliff face rising to their right and a steep slope of rocky shale dropping off sharply on the left. As a precaution, U.S. troops made it a habit never to take the same route into and out of an objective, and the trail wound around the valley and was just wide enough for a single pickup truck. Long-forgotten rains had washed it out in a number of places.

A late afternoon sun was still shining brightly on their slope, though the shadows were lengthening across the narrow canyon. On the winding path below, the U.S. soldiers spotted some of the men from Arenas following them, and then those men disappeared. Word came down the line to keep moving quickly and not stop. The patrol was entering a stretch with little cover and commanding heights above known as "ambush alley."

A single shot rang out, and patrol members swiveled around looking for its origin. Another shot echoed in the valley, and the entire patrol seemed to hold its breath. Then the whole valley ignited with muzzle flashes and the reports of automatic weapons fire from a three-pronged ambush, the attackers shooting down from the heights above. The patrol swung into action. Specialist White flipped his M4 on full automatic, and along with the other paratroopers blasted away at the nearest suspected enemy positions in a "mad minute" of suppressive fire. In less than half that time, he had emptied his thirty-round magazine, and in an oft-practiced gesture jettisoned it and locked in a fresh clip. He never even saw the rocket-propelled grenade hurtling toward his position, and then his world went black.

When Kyle White regained consciousness he was lying facedown on a rock in a concussion-induced fog. He tried lifting his head a few inches and an AK-47 round smacked off the rock inches away, sending rock shards splintering into his face. Just like that, White was suddenly wide awake, looking around with alarm to try to make sense of his surroundings. Most of his patrol had simply disappeared, sliding and tumbling down the shale cliff below in a desperate attempt to escape the enemy fire. As he turned around, White saw Specialist Kain Schilling stumbling down the trail ahead toward a small draw where their interpreter and some of the Afghan

Army soldiers were huddling for cover under the canopy of a tree. Even from a distance White could see that Schilling had been shot in the arm.

White got up and ran to the tree cover under fire, bullets ricocheting off the rocky ground at his feet. Catching his breath in the shade of the tree, he saw that the bullet had entered Schilling's right arm and exited through the top of his shoulder. He applied a tourniquet to stop his friend's bleeding, then dropped his heavy radio pack in order to start returning enemy fire. The tree didn't provide much cover, but in the shadows of its canopy the Taliban fighters couldn't draw an accurate bead on them.

Only something was wrong. White felt a burning in his chest and noticed a metallic taste in his mouth. Could the Afghan fighters somehow be using chemical weapons? Out of the corner of his eye, he saw that the radio pack was smoking. He realized that a bullet had pierced its lithium battery and started it burning, causing the acrid smell. Kain Schilling's radio had likewise been shot and destroyed. The American soldiers had no way to relay their position and desperate status to the rest of the patrol, let alone to their home base back at Camp Bella.

Then White noticed Marine Corps sergeant Phillip Bocks lying some thirty feet away, obviously badly wounded. He yelled for Bocks to try to crawl to the concealment of the tree, but the Marine was too badly hurt. White didn't want to leave Schilling, but he had to make a decision. His adrenaline was pumping on redline, his head pounding, but White was thinking clearly. Given the high volume and accuracy of enemy fire, and the lack of cover, he knew there was no way he was going to make it off that mountainside alive. It was just a matter of time before he was killed. And if he was going to die, Kyle White was determined to try to help his battle buddies until his last breath.

Before the thought even registered, White was in the open again and running toward Sergeant Bocks, feeling the pressure of the near misses as the bullets rent the air around his body.

Three times, Kyle White ran out to Bocks to drag the bigger man a little closer to cover, each time drawing so much enemy fire to them both that he had to break contact and try again. When White finally pulled the wounded Marine to cover he immediately began working on Bocks's wounds. He used a tourniquet to stop the bleeding from a bullet wound to Bocks's left leg, then cut off his uniform to bandage a wound to his shoulder. All the while, rounds were coming in close, hissing and cracking off the nearby rocks. Just as he had been trained, White kept checking for more wounds, and he discovered the large exit hole on Bocks's lower right rib cage, from which blood was flowing freely. White never stopped trying, but he sensed then that his friend was not going to make it. Soon after, Marine Corps Sergeant Phillip A. Bocks succumbed to his wounds.

White looked over his shoulder to the nearby tree canopy just in time to see Kain Schilling shot a second time, the bullet smashing into his left knee. Schilling cried out over the din of battle that he was hit again. Once again, White was up and running through fire, realizing only when he reached his friend that there were no more tourniquets to stop the bleeding from the fresh wound. Schilling's tourniquet was already wrapped around his arm, and White's was tied around Phillip Bocks's leg. So he ripped off his belt and cinched it around Shilling's upper thigh.

"Hey man, this is going to hurt!" White warned his friend.

"Just do it!" Schilling shouted as White put his foot on Schilling's leg and pulled as hard as he could.

After the bleeding stopped and Schilling was stabilized, White noticed that Lieutenant Matthew Ferrara was lying facedown on the trail ahead. He had to check on his commander, but the enemy fire was still too intense to make a run for it. So White high-crawled as fast as he could to reach Ferrara, checked his pulse, and confirmed that he had been killed. He then crawled to Bocks's body, desperately searching for a functional radio to relay their status and increasingly desperate position to base camp.

Finally, White experienced a moment of elation and even hope: Bocks's radio was still intact. He grabbed the hand microphone, and he was bringing it up to his head when an enemy bullet blew it right out of his hand. After everything that had happened, the sheer frustration and anger was overwhelming.

Really? White thought to himself. *Come on!*

Improbably, Bocks's radio still worked. White had trained as a radio operator, and he was able to switch it to walkie-talkie mode and for the first time relay their position and desperate status back to Camp Bella. He identified enemy positions and requested close air and indirect fire support to keep the Taliban from overrunning their position.

A short time later, U.S. artillery and mortar strikes began smashing down on enemy positions. In the midst of the bombardment, White heard a hissing sound way too close, and then a powerful blast knocked him to his knees. Going down, he could actually see fragments of hot metal the size of his fist hurtling past his body like a meteor shower. A 120mm round from a U.S. mortar had fallen short of its intended target and nearly finished what an entire Taliban ambush force had begun hours earlier.

Despite suffering his second concussion of the day, Kyle White was soon back on the radio relaying their position and status and requesting medivac helicopters. He was told it would take hours for the helicopters to reach their position. Through the Afghan interpreter, White directed the few Afghan soldiers who were not wounded to establish a security perimeter, guarding the trail from both directions. The sun was setting, and soon the mountainside disappeared into the pitch dark of a moonless night.

As the only able-bodied U.S. paratrooper still on the mountain, deep in enemy territory and half a world away from home, Kyle White felt alone as never before in his young life. The adrenaline of battle had worn off and he fought to stay awake through the pull of multiple concussions, knowing that if he passed out the medivac would never find them. He stared up into the night sky and saw the lights of U.S. military aircraft circling far above, and he found some solace there. Finally, one of the lights grew bigger, and soon a flight medic appeared at the end of a long cable to begin the arduous task of lifting the wounded and dead off the mountain. After they were all evacuated the cable descended a final time.

Specialist Kyle White was the last American off the mountainside.

White didn't know it, but base commanders all over Afghanistan had been glued to their radios throughout the battle, listening as a twenty-year-old paratrooper calmly called in enemy positions and organized a desperate defense while tending to his wounded comrades. Before the night was over, they would know him by his call sign, and recall it with deep respect in retelling the story: "Charlie One Six Romeo."

Kyle White was later awarded the Medal of Honor for his heroic actions that day, but years after transitioning to civilian life he would awake to the sights and sounds of that awful battle, thinking about the soldiers lost there. He wears a stainless steel bracelet around his wrist etched with the names of his six brothers in arms who died that day: Captain Matthew C. Ferrara, Sergeant Phillip A. Bocks, Sergeant Jeffrey S. Mersman, Corporal Lester G. Roque, Specialist Joseph M. Lancour, and Corporal Sean K. A. Langevin, Kyle White's best friend in the world.

"Nine November is a day that will be fresh in my mind for the rest of my life. I have no doubt, definitely something that day changed me as far as my chosen career," said White, who has been forthcoming about his struggles with post-traumatic stress. "You know, something changed that day and I can't even tell you what it is. It's not positive or negative. It's just that something was different."

Chapter 12

—☆—

The Natural

Army Staff Sergeant Robert J. Miller

The otherworldly mountains of northeast Kunar Province tower more than fourteen thousand feet above a landscape of steep river valleys and remote villages where life has changed little for hundreds of years. The tribes occupying some of the mud-hut dwellings had little contact with their neighbors in the next valley, let alone with the outside world. The Hindu Kush was country to get lost in, not control.

In late 2007 the Green Berets of Alpha Company, 3rd Battalion, 3rd Special Forces Group were inserted by helicopter into this remote mountainous region to make contact with villagers who had never before seen an American soldier. The mission was right out of the doctrinal handbook for the twelve-man Green Beret "A Team," or Operational Detachment Alpha (ODA), a self-contained fighting unit steeped in local cultures and languages and trained to team with indigenous forces in unconventional warfare.

For more than a week, Alpha Company commander Captain Robert Cusick and his team lived among Afghan villagers in the remote mountains of Kunar. They held free medical clinics for the locals as a part of a "hearts and minds" outreach, bringing along a female Army medic to treat the Afghan women. They were welcomed by village elders steeped in Pashtunwali, the code of conduct for Pashtun tribes that traces its origins back to the first millennium BC. It emphasizes hospitality and tolerance toward strangers. Captain Cusick and his soldiers held long talks with the elders to learn more about an area that straddled the "Durand Line," the mountainous, mostly invisible border between Afghanistan and Pakistan that traced its lineage back to the late 1800s and Sir Mortimer Durand, a former secretary of the British Indian government. The British and the empire they once claimed were long gone, and the line on a map that they drew was mostly ignored by the Pashtun tribes. The rugged mountains were crisscrossed by high passes, tunnels, and rocky goat trails, critical arteries linking Taliban insurgents in Afghanistan to sanctuary in nearby Pakistan.

"Are there any Taliban in this area?" Captain Cusick asked an elder through an interpreter.

"No, there are no Taliban here," the bearded, turbaned elder replied.

"Are you sure there are no Taliban?" Cusick repeated.

"There are no Taliban because we have never seen U.S. soldiers here before," the old man explained. "If U.S. soldiers don't come, the Taliban stay away. When you come, so will the Taliban."

On one of their last days in the village, the Special Forces soldiers looked on as the village men organized a game of Buzkashi, a rough-and-tumble Pashtun form of polo in which mounted horsemen compete to throw a goat carcass into an opposing team's "goal" that is scratched into the dirt. In the dusty scramble horses were toppled and men sometimes trampled beneath their hoofs, a dangerous dynamic made famous to Western audiences by the movie *Rambo III*.

A few of the Special Forces soldiers attempted to mount the wild and scrawny mountain horses to join in, but soon gave it up as a bad idea. Only Staff Sergeant Robert Miller, the youngest soldier in Alpha Company at just twenty-four years old, wasn't so easily discouraged. An athlete with the wiry frame of the standout gymnast that he had been in high school, Miller commandeered an Afghan horse and, once mounted, charged directly into the flailing scrum of men and horseflesh.

Already on his second tour in Afghanistan, with language skills that one of his teammates described as "off the charts," Miller was the best Pashto speaker on the A Team, and he spent much of his downtime with his Afghan counterparts to hone his fluency. Miller shouted and laughed as he wheeled the horse about and charged with his fellows in the Afghan light brigade. At one point he had to duck at the last second and hug his horse by the neck to avoid being knocked off by low-hanging tree branches, and his Green Beret teammates shouted and cheered. At that moment, in one the most remote locations on earth, young Robby Miller seemed more Lawrence of Arabia than Rambo. Which is to say he looked like the ideal of a Special Forces soldier.

"Being a medic I was waiting for Robby to fall when he went under those low branches, just in case he hurt himself, but after that I stood back and watched him play that horse game with the Afghans, and it was one of the coolest things I ever saw," recalled teammate Staff Sergeant Sergio Martinez. "He always spent time drinking tea and eating with the

Afghans after the day's work was done, while most of us were hanging with each other and just unwinding. So when he jumped on that horse and joined the Afghans in that game it was a unique moment. That's how I envision a Special Forces soldier acting. He set the standard that I held new team members to after that."

Robert Miller grew up one of eight siblings in the middle-class Chicago suburb of Wheaton, Illinois. On weekends his father would sometimes take Robby and his siblings to nearby Cantigny Park and the interactive First Division Museum and let them crawl over the armored behemoths in the museum's iconic tank park, which spans a hundred years of military history. Phil Miller had served a tour in the U.S. Army in the early 1980s, and had been stationed in West Berlin during the height of the Cold War. An abiding interest in the U.S. military ran through the family, evident in the library of military history books that Phil had inherited from an uncle.

As part of a grade school project, young Robby had even penned a poem about American soldiers during the Battle of the Bulge: "Men who fought day and night, fighting for what they thought was right."

As a young boy Robby would also accompany his mother, Maureen, when she did volunteer work visiting the homes of Cambodian refugees and teaching them English. Some of his first friends were the children of those refugees who had escaped the Khmer Rouge genocide. Because he showed an interest, Maureen even allowed Robby to see the movie *The Killing Fields*, which dramatized that atrocity, when he was just a boy. He learned at a young age what can befall a people at the mercy of cruel tyrants.

"I think that made a real impression on Robby," Maureen Miller told the author in an interview. "I also think his keen interest in foreign languages and cultures came from that early experience. He got a kick out of learning curse words in Cambodian that I couldn't understand!"

In high school Robby Miller became a leader on the gymnastics team. He kept a pommel horse in his garage and trained relentlessly. Though he was in many ways a typical happy-go-lucky teenager, his gymnastics coach noticed a serious streak and fierce determination that only grew over time and set Miller apart. Robby also became fascinated by Ernest Hemingway's books and their depiction of men who adopted a personal code that valued courage and grace under pressure above nearly all else.

After high school Robert Miller enrolled at the University of Iowa, but when his hope of walking on to the gymnastics team wasn't realized, he began looking seriously at joining the U.S. Army instead. He enlisted in March 2003, shortly after the 9/11 terrorist attacks and during the U.S. invasion of Iraq. There was no doubt in Robert Miller's mind that he was volunteering to go to war, a likelihood that became a certainty when he joined an "18 X-Ray" program that fast-tracked standout recruits for membership in the legendary Green Berets of U.S. Army Special Forces.

"Robby became really serious about joining the U.S. military when he was a freshman in college, but it didn't come as a surprise to any of us," said Maureen Miller. "Looking back, I believe he was heading toward the military from the day he was born."

Heavy snows already blanketed the operating base in Kunar Province in December 2007 when Alpha Company received a "warning order" of heavy activity in a suspected Taliban winter stronghold in the vicinity of the Chen Khar Valley. The location was significant both symbolically and strategically. During the Red Army's decade-long war in Afghanistan in the 1980s, the deep valley summits and well-fortified positions of the area provided a safe haven for Afghan mujahedeen, protecting their supply lines into Pakistan. The Red Army was never able to dislodge the guerrillas. Recent U.S. surveillance and reconnaissance operations suggested that a number of high-value Taliban commanders had massed their forces in the valley and its three surrounding villages to shelter during the winter.

The warning order arrived during a period of inflection in the Afghan War. After more than six years and $120 billion toward nation building in a time of insurgency in Afghanistan, evidence was mounting that the United States and its allies in the International Security Assistance Force (ISAF) had at best fought the Taliban to a stalemate. Already 2007 was the deadliest year yet for allied troops fighting in Afghanistan, with the number of roadside bombs increasing dramatically and incidents of "indirect fire" that included suicide bombings nearly doubling.

After regrouping in uncontested sanctuary in nearby Pakistan, the Taliban had seized and held the district of Musa Qala in Afghanistan's southern Helmand Province for nine months in 2007, before the Afghan Army and its ISAF allies were finally able to retake the province in December. After a series of tactical victories over Afghan security forces, however, the Taliban's confidence and morale were spiking dramatically. At the time the U.S. military was focusing the overwhelming majority of its manpower and military resources on Iraq. After denying an urgent request for fifty thousand more troops from the top U.S. commander in Afghanistan, Chairman of the Joint Chiefs of Staff Admiral Michael Mullen explained on December 11, 2007, "In Afghanistan, we do what we can. In Iraq, we do what we must."

The deteriorating strategic situation in Afghanistan was evident in the video display maps in the 3rd Special Forces Group's tactical operations center. In an earlier deployment in 2006–7, the group's base was surrounded by "white space" on the map designating a largely secure environment. Single vehicles traveled freely, and soldiers attended weddings and dinners with their Afghan counterparts without bothering about extra security. By early 2008 the surrounding white space had turned a cautionary "yellow," designating possible enemy activity. The Afghan troops U.S. Special Forces had trained and bonded with on the deployment just a year earlier were gone, an indication of an extremely high turnover in the ranks of the Afghan National Army that would bedevil ISAF commanders for the duration of the war.

By late January 2008, Alpha Company had its orders: U.S. air forces were going to strike the suspected Taliban winter headquarters in Gowardesh, in the vicinity of Chen Khar. Alpha Company and an accompanying Afghan Army unit would mount a combat reconnaissance patrol to conduct bomb damage assessment after the strike.

On the night of January 25, 2008, Staff Sergeants Robert Miller and Nicholas McGarry, the company's two "weapons sergeants," were busy preparing their teammates for the night's mission: handing out extra batteries for night-vision devices, sighting laser rangefinders on individual weapons, and issuing fire suppressors to mask the muzzle flashes of their M4 automatic rifles at night. There was none of the typical bitching or moaning that sometimes accompanied operations. Alpha Company was focused on a mission they all understood was perilous.

In a quiet moment leading up to the mission, Robby Miller and Nick McGarry talked about the one subject that no soldiers in a war zone can escape. McGarry had a few years on Miller, but as the two youngest soldiers and the weapons experts in the company they had forged a close bond. Back at Fort Bragg, North Carolina, they were the single guys in the unit who rented bachelor pads next to each other, and on some nights after work drank beers and sang karaoke together at one of the local dives. There was a goofy, fun-loving side to Robby Miller when he was off duty that stood in marked contrast to the seriousness he displayed in the field, and McGarry loved him for it.

"You know, if I die I want you guys to celebrate my life, who I was and what I did, not mourn my loss," Miller told his friend, and McGarry seconded the emotion. "I wouldn't want everyone to sit around crying. If it comes to that, throw a party and laugh and tell stories about the funny things and good times we had."

The convoy of armored Humvees and Toyota pickup trucks snaked through a pitch-dark vortex of towering rock, snow, and bitter wind. There was only one road in and out of the steep valley, meaning the Taliban were unlikely to have booby-trapped it with improvised explosive devices lest they cut off their own supply line. On their left a sheer rock wall climbed into the unseen heights, and to their right down an embankment, river waters churned around snow- and ice-covered boulders. Another rock face rose beyond the river. Maneuver was out of the question.

Staff Sergeant McGarry manned the .50 caliber machine gun in the first gun truck turret and peered into the darkness straight ahead. In the Humvee just behind, Staff Sergeant Miller swiveled his Mk 19 automatic grenade launcher to protect the rear of the column. At a bend in the river, McGarry was first to see the boulders blocking the road. Immediately they understood that the Taliban were very near.

At the insistence of a senior sergeant on their first deployment to Afghanistan, both Miller and McGarry had read *The Bear Went Over the Mountain: Soviet Combat Tactics in Afghanistan*, a compendium of the lessons learned by Red Army commanders who fought a decade-long, losing war against the Afghan mujahedeen in the 1980s. Placing boulders and other obstacles in the road to slow the advance and reveal an approaching enemy was a favorite ambush tactic of Afghan insurgents.

After they twice cleared boulders from the road with explosives, Staff Sergeant Miller organized a dismounted overwatch element of Afghan National Army soldiers, who trudged through the snow and wind to protect the convoy's flanks against ambush. Finally, lead elements of the convoy rounded another bend and could see the objective—a chokepoint across the river where the valley narrowed into a steep canyon. A surveillance drone confirmed the presence of an estimated fifteen to twenty insurgents occupying dug-in fighting positions three to four hundred yards into the valley.

The convoy soon started taking machine-gun and automatic weapons fire from that direction. McGarry opened up with the .50 caliber, and Miller jumped back into the Humvee and engaged enemy positions with his grenade launcher while expertly relaying enemy coordinates to an Air Force tactical air controller. Soon thunder filled the valley as first two F-15 Strike Eagles swooped overhead and made strafing runs with their large-caliber Gatling guns. The Strike Eagles were followed by two A-10 Warthog close air support aircraft on a second devastating strafing run.

In the midst of the firepower display, Miller's grenade launcher malfunctioned, so he abandoned it and kept firing with an M240B machine gun mounted on the rear of the Humvee, continuing to call out enemy positions to the tactical air controller. Deafening explosions and blinding fireballs erupted on the mountainside as three precision-guided 500-pound bombs fell on the dug-in Taliban fighting positions. After the rocks and debris settled the valley was quiet as death.

With surveillance platforms detecting no further movement around enemy positions, Captain Cusick directed a dismounted patrol of some fifteen Afghan soldiers and eight U.S. Special Forces troops to conduct a battle damage assessment. Surely little could have survived the devastating display of airpower. Given his fluency in Pashto and cool actions under fire, Staff Sergeant Robby Miller was chosen to lead the patrol as point.

The Afghan and U.S. Special Forces soldiers crossed the Gowardesh Bridge in single file and trudged quietly up the valley through snowdrifts and swirling wind. Miller paused for a moment and sat down to clear something out of his boot, and Staff Sergeant McGarry stepped up to walk point. Less than a minute later McGarry felt a tap on the shoulder and turned to see the face of his best friend, who was carrying an M249 Squad Automatic Weapon, the heaviest firepower on the patrol.

"It's all right, Nick," Robby Miller said. "I've got this."

☆ ☆ ☆

The steep mountainsides closed in as the patrol entered a copse of trees at the mouth of a narrow gorge, and Sergeant Miller signaled to the Afghan soldiers to fan out into a fighting formation. Through the night-vision goggles the scene seemed peaceful and eerily silent.

"Allahu akbar!" The shout pierced the quiet and echoed in the narrow gorge as an insurgent stepped out from behind a boulder and fired his AK-47 from just a few yards away. Miller cut the man down with a burst from his SAW. The traditional call of the mujahedeen warrior of "God is great!" initiated the ambush, and insurgents in fighting positions dug into the canyon walls on three sides opened up with machine guns and rocket-propelled grenades. Straight ahead on the valley floor a handful of Taliban insurgents and a PKM machine-gun crew were firing from behind boulders and trees. Just like that the patrol was caught in a kill zone with little cover and no chance to organize an orderly retreat.

To the Green Berets the intensity of fire from the surrounding hillsides looked like the sparkle of flashbulbs in a concert stadium at night, each flash a deadly spit of flame. Snow geysers erupted everywhere at the impact of countless bullets. Afghan soldiers at the head of the patrol were trying to pull back, and some ran, but the Taliban machine gun cut them down. Grasping the dire need of his comrades, Robby Miller charged forward and poured suppressive fire into the machine-gun nest until it was silenced. He swiveled and engaged other enemy positions to give his teammates a chance to retreat and regroup.

"I'm hit! I'm hit!" The call rang out over the open radio frequency, and all of the Special Forces troops recognized the voice of their commander, Captain Cusick, hit by a bullet that struck his left shoulder from above and then punctured a lung. A few of the Green Berets scrambled to try and pull their captain to safety as he coughed up blood, exposing themselves to enemy fire. The order was given to fall back and find cover.

At that moment Robby Miller made a fateful decision. Giving his teammates a chance to pull back and render aid to their wounded commander, he once again moved forward alone, training the SAW on multiple enemy positions with deadly accuracy. In the dark each burst of his unsuppressed machine gun lit the ghastly scene like a blowtorch, drawing insurgent fire onto his position and giving his teammates precious seconds to find cover.

An unseen insurgent shot Miller as he was engaged with another enemy position, the bullet striking him under the right arm where the body armor ended. He turned and killed the man, and continued fighting. Critically wounded and separated from his teammates, Miller low-crawled forward through blood-streaked snow, firing uphill at enemy positions on the hillsides and drawing enemy fire away from his wounded commander and teammates. He was hit and wounded a second time under his left arm, and still he kept firing.

As they regrouped behind a rock wall and a medic tended to Captain Cusick, Miller's teammates could hear him continue to identify enemy positions over the radio, and then they heard that he was hit. The insurgent fire around his position was so intense and kicked up so much snow and debris that they could no longer see Robby Miller with their night vision, but the percussive explosion of his grenades rumbled in the valley three times, and the angry rattle of the SAW rent the night until all of his ammunition was spent and finally the big gun fell silent.

The first two Green Berets to reach Robby Miller's body were hit with intense small-arms fire that struck their body armor and ricocheted off their equipment, forcing them to break contact and scramble to take cover. After a quick reaction force of reinforcements arrived, other ODA team members led the group back into the narrow gorge to try and recover Miller. In the midst of the recovery operation a rocket-propelled grenade landed in the middle of the soldiers, spraying a number of them with jagged shrapnel. Others were hit by small-arms fire, forcing the quick reaction force to establish a second casualty collection point and call in more medivac helicopters. Soon

Apache helicopter gunships were conducting strafing runs with their 30mm chain guns to try and suppress the deadly Taliban fire.

By the time Alpha Company recovered Miller's body and trudged back across the Gowardesh Bridge, only three of the original eight members were unscathed by bullets or shrapnel. The post-battle intelligence assessment estimated that the U.S. and Afghan National Army soldiers had encountered a well-fortified, company-sized force of more than 140 Taliban fighters. Sergeant Miller is believed to have killed more than 16 insurgents and wounded over 30 more, undoubtedly saving the lives of teammates with his self-sacrifice.

Months later at a memorial service for Robert Miller held at Fort Bragg, his parents, Phil and Maureen, were presented with a handmade Afghan rug with his name and unit designation woven beautifully into the fabric. The Afghan soldiers he trained and befriended were devastated by the loss of the American who spoke their language, loved their culture, and died fighting for their country. So they pooled their paltry pay and commissioned the rug as an act of gratitude and remembrance. Today it hangs in a place of honor in Phil and Maureen Miller's living room.

As to why young Robby Miller decided to push forward into the face of enemy fire and almost certain death when the order was to pull back, that was a topic of considerable discussion among his surviving teammates.

"It came down to when we were pulling back, Sergeant Miller was moving forward. We'll never know exactly why, but my personal opinion was he wanted to give cover for his buddies to pull back," said Captain Robert Cusick, the A Team commander who was badly wounded in the battle. "But to this day I don't know why he did it. Maybe when I meet my maker, I'll get to sit down with Robby and talk about it."

Chapter 13

———☆———

Shok Valley

Army Staff Sergeant Ronald J. Shurer II

Army Sergeant Matthew O. Williams

My leg doesn't feel right."

"Look, man, you're going to be okay," Staff Sergeant Ron Shurer told his Special Forces teammate as he felt around the soldier's pelvis and discovered the small entry hole of the bullet, oozing blood to the fluttering rhythm of the man's heart. "Just let me take care of this wound first."

They lay on a small ledge in the shadow of an enemy compound some sixty feet above. At the edge a cliff face dropped sixty feet to the valley below. There was little cover, and constant fire from the compound and from across the narrow valley screeched off the rock wall and kicked up dirt geysers in every direction. Their young Afghan interpreter, Edris Khan, nicknamed "CK" by the Green Berets who had adopted him almost as a little brother, lay lifeless against the cliff wall where his blood and gore were splattered. Radioman and staff sergeant Luis Morales was crumpled in a heap where a round into his thigh had smashed him to the ground like a sledgehammer, and another bullet had torn open his ankle. Senior Airman Zach Rhyner, the joint terminal attack controller responsible for calling in air support, was sitting by a small tree with his back to the enemy compound, seemingly in a daze. Team leader Captain Kyle Walton was pressed against the cliff wall talking frantically into a radio as other troopers tried vainly to suppress the fire raining down on the ledge from multiple directions. Everything was decidedly not okay.

Special Forces medics are detached and coldly calculating by training, the better to prepare them to quickly conduct triage on multiple casualties. As the lone medic for Operational Detachment Alpha 3336, Ron Shurer had to decide in the heat of battle which of his teammates were likely to survive their wounds, and who would die without immediate care. Shurer returned his attention to Staff Sergeant Dillon Behr's pelvic wound, a difficult-to-reach vascular injury that was bleeding at an alarming rate. If they didn't find a way to get him off that cliff ledge soon, Behr was surely going to lapse into shock and die.

"Just keep pressure on this wound as hard as you can," Shurer told Specialist Michael Carter, a combat cameraman drafted into emergency medical duty. The medic then injected Behr with morphine and packed the wound with gauze and Celox, a blood-clotting agent.

"You're going to be fine. It's no big deal," Shurer assured Behr, and then turned to shout to Captain Walton over the din of battle. "We need to get him out of here now!"

Shurer was startled to feel Dillon Behr grabbing his arm.

"So you're telling him I'm going to die, and you're telling me I'm okay, right?" Behr said.

There was no way the medic was going to tell Behr the truth and risk the soldier giving up on himself. Yet since the Special Forces detachment was trapped in a kill zone on that exposed ledge with little cover and enemy fire pouring down from the heights, and the seriously wounded were piling up by the minute, it would surely take a miracle to get Behr or the rest of them off that mountain alive. Their dire predicament was captured in great detail in the riveting book *No Way Out*, by Mitch Weiss and Kevin Maurer.

"You're fine," Ron Shurer reassured his friend once again.

Earlier that morning their flight of six Chinook helicopters had banked through the gathering clouds and descended into the Shok Valley, a deep gash in the Hindu Kush so remote and impenetrable that the Soviet army had avoided it during a decade of war against Afghan guerrillas. The three Special Forces "A" teams and a company of Afghan commandos on board the lumbering troop carriers were on a "capture or kill" mission searching for Haji Ghafour, a high-ranking commander with the Hezb-e Islami Gulbuddin (HIG) terrorist group. A Taliban affiliate that had recently formed an alliance with Al Qaeda, HIG was responsible for a series of increasingly brazen attacks on U.S. and allied forces that would make 2008 a pivotal year in the long Afghan War.

Everyone understood that it was a high-risk mission for a top-tier target, and the thin margins of error for success began to shrink even before the lumbering Chinooks touched down. As soon as the helicopter formation broke through the cloud cover, aircrews could see that there were hundreds more mud-brick buildings clinging to the steep hillsides than were evident from aerial surveillance video. The enemy force was likely to prove far larger than they anticipated.

The intelligence on the topography was also wrong. The landing zone where the mammoth helicopters were supposed to set down to discharge troops lay at the confluence of three steep ravines, and it was a porcupine's back of jagged rocks and boulders beside a rushing river swollen by the melting snows of early April. The gathering clouds also threatened to envelop the entire valley, potentially making medical evacuation or extraction difficult, if not impossible.

For Captain Kyle Walton and Master Sergeant Scott Ford, who as leaders of Operational Detachment Alpha (ODA) 3336 were designated as the main effort in the operation, the plan itself felt all wrong. Originally their idea was for the helicopters to drop them on the ridgeline above the target compound by fast rope, so the Special Forces troops and Afghan commandos could approach the village from the all-important high ground. Because the 101st Airborne Division helicopter pilots were new in theater and relatively unfamiliar with the conditions, higher command decided instead that they would drop the troops on the valley floor, in daylight. That fateful decision determined that they would be fighting uphill, likely against an entrenched enemy operating on his home turf, with little hope of surprise.

"Our plan," Walton later told a *Washington Post* reporter, "was to fight downhill."

Unwilling to set down on the jagged rocks in the riverbed, the first Chinook hovered some ten feet above the ground as the heavily laden Green Berets and Afghan commandos jumped out the rear into the freezing river below. After the last helicopter lifted off and disappeared into the clouds, nearly everyone in the assembled task force was struck by the eerie quiet of the Shok Valley. No baying of goats or distant noises of a mountain village coming to life in the morning. Not even the sound of birds. The silence seemed unnatural, like a held breath.

The target compound was a village of mud-brick buildings perched on the terraced mountainside, clearly visible from the valley floor and accessible only by a single, zigzagging path of switchbacks suitable for pack mules and little else. The satellite images everyone had studied failed to do justice to the sheer scale and steepness of the mountains.

As Captain Walton and the lead element of ODA 3336 set off up the mule path, members noticed Specialist Carter snapping photos of the mountains.

"Man, they're beautiful," he said, and no one disagreed.

"Ron! Ron! Ron! Ron! Ron!"

Staff Sergeant Ron Shurer heard his name echo in the valley, carried on the voices of Afghan commandos as they cowered behind whatever cover they could find. The fusillade of machine-gun and sniper fire and rocket-propelled grenades was thunderous. Hearing a chorus of Afghans shouting his name, Shurer knew that Staff Sergeant Ryan Wallen was likely hit. Wallen had instructed all of his Afghan trainees to call for the medic if he was ever injured.

Shurer reached his injured teammate and inspected his neck wound. There was significant blood, but the medic quickly determined that there was no vascular damage, and the soldier's airways looked clear. Wallen would be all right. As he was wrapping the wound in gauze, both soldiers heard a frantic call over the radio net from Captain Walton. Behr, Morales, and CK had all been hit by enemy fire, and they needed the medic up on the mountainside now.

"Did you hear that?" Wallen said.

"Yeah, I heard it," said Shurer.

"I'm good. Go get them," said Wallen.

But Shurer didn't know how he could possibly make it up the mountainside alive given the intensity of the enemy fire. Medics are trained not to expose themselves to fire except in dire need, so as not to deprive the team of its chief medical expert. Nevertheless he prepared to cross several hundred meters of contested ground to reach his pinned-down teammates, running a gauntlet of enemy fire. The young medic's pedigree demanded nothing less.

After the September 11, 2001, terrorist attacks on the United States, Ronald J. Shurer was inspired to join a long line of family members who had answered the call to military duty. His great-grandfather, grandfather, and both parents had served in the U.S. armed forces, and he grew up as the only son of an Air Force couple. With a bachelor's degree from Washington State University, he joined the Army in 2002 and was assigned to a Medical Support Battalion at Fort Bragg, North Carolina, home to U.S. Army Special Forces. Following completion of the difficult Special Forces Qualification Course in 2004, Shurer donned his green beret and in 2006 reported to duty with the 3rd Special Forces Group. He was already on his second tour in Afghanistan, but nothing quite prepared him for what his team encountered in the Shok Valley on April 6, 2008.

The HIG fighters were not some ragtag band of Taliban, firing blindly from behind cover in an undisciplined spray of bullets. They had waited patiently until the U.S. and Afghan commandos were spread out and picking their way up the narrow mountain trail before springing their ambush, and their fire was intense and deadly accurate.

Weapons Sergeant Nick McGarry was in a supporting fire team whose mission was to scale the opposite mountainside and provide machine-gun cover for ODA 3336's ascent. When the lead element was hit hard they changed plans and tried to reach Captain Walton and his men directly.

"Where Captain Walton and ODA 3336 got hit was very steep and at the top of a terraced, hundred-foot cliff," McGarry said in an interview with the author. "Everyone was being hit with plunging fire from elevated enemy positions. I had rounds landing between my legs. Two of the Afghan commandos in my team were hit, and my teammate Eric Martin was shot in the leg. We tried to cross the valley to reach the foot of the cliff three times, and three times we were repelled by really intense machine-gun and sniper fire."

★ ★ ★

Weapons Sergeant Matthew Williams was pinned down on the valley floor when he heard over the radio net that Captain Walton and the lead element had sustained multiple casualties and were in acute danger of being overrun. He quickly gathered a group of Afghan commandos and, despite the intense enemy fire, led them in a counterattack as they hopscotched around ice-covered boulders. At the foot of the mountain they started to climb.

At one switchback Williams ran into Master Sergeant Scott Ford and Staff Sergeant Ron Shurer trudging up the same mule trail, where they had stopped only to scramble for cover or help each other scale the steep terraces. The timing of the encounter was a rare bit of good luck on an otherwise dark day. Above them a group of HIG fighters were moving into firing positions to possibly flank and overrun Captain Walton's team and cut off any rescue. Williams and Ford swung their M4 rifles around and dropped the insurgents in a burst of fire. They resumed climbing, and, cresting a final ridge, Sergeants Ford, Shurer, and Williams reached the ledge where their teammates were trapped. If anything, the situation was even worse than they feared.

Sergeant Dillon Behr was drifting away, his mind and body succumbing to the painkillers and massive loss of blood, until he was yanked back to harsh reality by a slap across his face.

"Wake up, Dillon!" Ron Shurer shouted, determined that his friend not lapse into shock. "You're not going to die today!"

Shurer had his fingers shoved inside Behr's pelvic wound, waiting for the Celox agent to mix with red blood cells and form the clotting gel that would hopefully stop the hemorrhaging. The medic had just performed a similar procedure on Morales, who was in nearly as bad a shape. In the background, Shurer could hear Captain Walton and the Combat Controller, Rhyner, calling in airstrikes on the compound just over their heads to suppress the deadly enemy fire. Nearby lay the body of their friend and Afghan interpreter. In their desperation the U.S. commandos used his lifeless body to provide cover for the wounded.

His hand still inside Behr's wound, Shurer heard a scream, and swiveled his head in time to see Staff Sergeant John Wayne Walding knocked through the air. The sniper round nearly severed his right leg just below the knee. Shurer's immediate instinct was to run to Walding, but until the Celox gelled that might condemn Behr. The medic saw a fellow soldier apply a tourniquet to the traumatic leg wound, and he went back to administering to Behr until finally he heard Walding shout out in pain and fear.

"Ron, you want to check me out, man?!" Walding shouted.

"You're good," Shurer shouted back, his hand still stuffed in Behr's pelvic wound.

"Are you kidding me?" Walding replied in disbelief, as recounted in *No Way Out*. "That's bullshit. Don't tell me I'm good. Fuck you, I'm good. I have no fucking leg!"

Minutes later two rounds struck Captain Walton in the helmet, mashing his face into the ground. Another bullet grazed Shurer's arm. Master Sergeant Ford was hit in the chest and knocked nearly to the ground, but the bullet failed to penetrate his body armor. The next round passed through Ford's left arm and shoulder before hitting Shurer in the helmet like a baseball bat. Matthew Williams broke cover and ran through the increasingly accurate enemy fire to render aid to Ford.

An obviously dazed Shurer tried to check himself and saw that he was covered in blood. He looked at Behr. "I just got shot!" the disoriented medic shouted. "Am I all right?"

The HIG snipers were zeroing in on the Green Berets.

The shock wave and eruption from the 2,000-pound bomb swallowed all light, rocks and debris raining onto the heads of the assault team pinned down on the ledge. Wounded and desperate, Master Sergeant Ford had devised a plan for getting them off the mountain. By now F-15 fighter aircraft were streaking repeatedly through the valley and dropping bombs "danger close" on the village just above their heads. Every time a bomb dropped, the Green Berets took advantage of the brief respite in enemy fire to lower one of the casualties to the terrace below, hopscotching them down the mountain. In a moment of inspiration, Ron Shurer had wrapped the casualties in tubular nylon webbing the U.S. commandos carried with their supplies and used it to lower them down to the next terrace.

When they reached the casualty collection point the group

was still taking intense enemy fire from the heights above. Staff Sergeant Shurer still offered encouragement as he moved among the many wounded.

"You're good. Don't die."

After helping to evacuate a wounded Master Sergeant Ford down the mountain, Sergeant Williams climbed back up the mountainside under heavy enemy fire to provide covering fire and assist the evacuation of other wounded. By the time he returned to the casualty collection point, Williams had the thousand-yard stare common to soldiers in intense, extended combat. They had been fighting outnumbered for more than six hours, and half the Green Berets were wounded, four of them critically. Together with the Afghan commandos they had suffered fifteen wounded and two killed, both of them Afghans.

The first Black Hawk medical evacuation helicopter appeared and descended just over the heads of the group at the casualty collection point, but its rotors were immediately hit by enemy fire and the pilot swerved away. A second medivac helicopter landed more than a hundred yards away on the other side of the icy river. Those Green Berets who were still ambulatory made a mad dash for it, carrying or assisting the many casualties across the water. The medivac pilots stoically waited for the group as bullets pinged off their fuselage.

"I was basically carrying Morales, whose foot was all but shot off, and Master Sergeant Ford was hanging on to me for support as we waded thigh deep through the frigid water," Sergeant Nick McGarry recalled in an interview. "We loaded so many wounded into that helicopter that the onboard medic almost pulled his shoulder out trying to keep them all from falling out when the helicopter took off."

After the medivac carrying the wounded disappeared, Captain Walton and the remaining assault team members counted heads and then fought a rearguard action farther down the valley to reach their exfiltration point. Bad weather was closing in and the clouds could soon make extraction impossible, and no one wanted to spend the night in that accursed valley. The pilots providing close air support overhead reported seeing more than a hundred HIG fighters still moving toward Walton and his team, likely bent on revenge for the estimated 150 to 200 of their comrades killed in many hours of intense fighting. The time had come to leave the Shok Valley behind, though the scars of April 6, 2008, would endure a lifetime.

For their heroism in battle, ten members of Operational Detachment Alpha 3336, 3rd Special Forces Group received the Silver Star, the U.S. military's third-highest decoration for valor. It was the highest number given for a single battle since the Vietnam War. The recipients were Captain Kyle Walton, Sergeant First Class Scott Ford, Staff Sergeant Luis Morales, Staff Sergeant Seth Howard, Staff Sergeant John Walding, Staff Sergeant Dillon Behr, Staff Sergeant David Sanders, Specialist Michael Carter, Sergeant Matthew Williams, and Staff Sergeant Ronald Shurer.

Remarkably, not a single American soldier died in the Battle of Shok Valley. There are a number of reasons why U.S. soldiers wounded in Afghanistan and Iraq were more likely to survive than their counterparts in any previous war, including body armor, advances in combat medicine and techniques such as easy-to-use field tourniquets, advanced blood-clotting medicines, and increased training for treating hemorrhaging. The Battle of Shok Valley suggests a further explanation why no American soldier died that day—the expertise, training, and valor of a determined combat medic, and the heroism of U.S. soldiers willing to repeatedly risk their own lives to save a wounded buddy. Both Staff Sergeant Ron Shurer and Sergeant Matthew Williams would receive the Medal of Honor, the nation's highest award for valor, for their actions on April 6, 2008.

"Ron Shurer had an impossible feat ahead of him. Dillon Behr wouldn't have lasted 10, 20 minutes with his injuries. Because of Ron, he lasted six or seven hours," Sergeant Mathew Williams later recalled the actions of his fellow awardee in an interview with *Army Times*. "Ron always was that guy, but it really came to light during the worst possible time. And that is the reason that we were able to make it away from that position alive, as a team."

"Obviously no one wants a day like this," Shurer recalled in an interview. "You want to go in, succeed easily, go home, and talk about how tough we were. This day was not like anything we'd seen before. Luckily, I relied on past experiences and training to get everyone through it."

Chapter 14

——☆——

The Ranger Creed

Army Staff Sergeant Leroy A. Petry

The helicopters carrying Army Rangers of the 75th Ranger Regiment flew in low and fast, the rocky landscape below unspooling in a liquid blur. Launching a helicopter assault against a well-guarded compound in broad daylight was extremely high-risk, but those were the type of missions that tended to get assigned to the 75th Rangers. The D Company, 2nd Battalion soldiers who were hurtling across eastern Afghanistan at midday on May 26, 2008, bore the same unit designation as the 75th Rangers who famously scaled hundred-foot cliffs under intense German fire at Pointe du Hoc on D-Day in 1944. In the more than half century that had passed since the Allied invasion that signaled the beginning of the end of World War II, nothing had changed in their creed: "Rangers Lead the Way."

Staff Sergeant Leroy Petry was on his seventh combat deployment, a whirlwind of fighting that was foreshadowed in his first weeks of tough Ranger training when an instructor entered their class on the morning of September 11, 2001, and told the soldiers, "Keep training, you might be going to war." Within months, Petry and his fellow Rangers were in Afghanistan helping lead the way. Seven years later Petry was still fighting, with two tours in Iraq under his belt and back yet again in Afghanistan, an infantryman's war if ever there was one.

Petry was where he wanted to be. As a young boy growing

up in New Mexico he would stare at the pictures hanging on the wall of their home showing his dashing grandfathers and uncles in uniform. He believed even then that soldiering would be his calling too. After graduating from Saint Catherine's Indian High School he worked for a time with his father and grandfather in the maintenance department at Pecos Public Transportation, but he was restless. In 1998, he walked into a U.S. Army recruiting station in New Mexico and enlisted, later volunteering for the 75th Ranger Regiment because it was known as among the best. In his time in the Rangers, Petry had served as a grenadier, squad automatic rifleman, fire team leader, and squad leader.

By the spring of 2008, Staff Sergeant Leroy Petry was a twenty-eight-year-old soldier with a wife and four young kids waiting anxiously for his return back home to New Mexico. But looking around, he knew that he was also needed in Afghanistan. As Petry put it, "These are my brothers—family just like my wife and kids—and you protect the ones you love."

The helicopters flared and settled in a blinding cloud of dust north and south of the primary target, a large walled compound thought to house a senior Al Qaeda commander. The rare daylight assault had been approved out of concern that the terrorist chief was only there temporarily. Once on the ground, Petry led a squad through a breach in the outer courtyard wall, and the group moved quickly through to clear the main building in a practiced choreography. Petry and Private First Class Lucas Robinson then returned to the courtyard and moved across to secure an outbuilding used as a chicken coop.

The sudden impact felt like a hammer slamming into Petry's leg. The Al Qaeda fighter had crept to only ten yards away, and the 7.62mm bullet actually passed through both of his legs, miraculously failing to strike an artery or bone. Another round struck Robinson in the side plate of his body armor. Badly wounded but juiced by the adrenaline of battle, Petry hustled Robinson to cover behind the nearby chicken coop and collapsed against a wall. They were in a close-quarters firefight with two insurgents, AK-47 rounds slamming into the walls and tearing off chunks of the flimsy structure. Sergeant Petry radioed that two Rangers were wounded and in contact with the enemy in the outer courtyard.

Sergeant Daniel Higgins entered the courtyard next just outside the line of fire. Petry grabbed a thermobaric grenade, pulled the pin, and lobbed it over the roof of the chicken coop toward the insurgents on the other side. The explosion momentarily silenced the enemy fire and allowed Higgins to sprint across the open ground and come to their aid. As Higgins checked their wounds, an enemy grenade landed not ten meters away. They clenched and then the blast knocked the three Rangers to the ground, sending searing shards of shrapnel into both Higgins and Robinson. They were in a fight to the death with only a chicken coop separating them from the enemy.

Staff Sergeant James Roberts and Specialist Christopher

Gathercole entered the outer courtyard and moved forward, firing, to relieve their friends. Then another grenade landed at the feet of the three Rangers. Despite the severity of his wounds, Leroy Petry lunged for the grenade and in a single motion tried to toss it around the corner of the chicken coop away from Higgins and Robinson. The ear-shattering detonation ripped Petry's right hand off at the wrist and splattered his arms and legs with shrapnel.

Stunned from the blast and the sight of his mutilated arm, Petry fought to stay focused. The younger Rangers would take their cue from the squad leader, and their lives at that moment depended on him staying calm. Petry quickly applied his own tourniquet to stanch the bleeding in his maimed arm, and then reported over the radio that he had been wounded again and the group was still in contact with the enemy. He directed his soldiers to maintain the defense and stay in the fight. Staff Sergeant James Roberts furiously fired his M4 rifle, keeping the enemy on the other side of the chicken coop at bay. Another insurgent appeared at the east end of the courtyard and opened fire, dropping Specialist Gathercole. Higgins and Robinson returned fire and cut him down.

Sergeant First Class Jerod Staidle and platoon medic Specialist Gary Depriest reached the group and began assessing their injuries. Petry calmly described his wounds to the medic. Peppered by shrapnel, missing his right hand, and shot through both legs, he was hurt as badly as any of them had seen short of death. Reinforcements arrived and killed the remaining insurgents, and Sergeant Daniel Higgins helped

Petry to the casualty collection point. Higgins was sure that both he and Private Robinson were alive only because of Petry's selfless act in grabbing the grenade.

As Petry's stretcher was being loaded onto the medivac helicopter, one of his teammates came over and shook his remaining hand. "That was the first time I shook the hand of someone who I consider to be a true American hero," the Ranger would later say. Staff Sergeant Petry "showed that true heroes still exist, and that they're closer than you think."

Despite losing a hand and suffering wounds to his legs that at times made it hard for him to stand, Leroy Petry later chose to reenlist indefinitely, and even returned to Afghanistan for an eighth deployment with his fellow Rangers. He was later assigned to the headquarters of the 75th Ranger Regiment at Fort Benning, Georgia, where he helped counsel and inspire other wounded warriors. For his own inspiration, Petry keeps a small plaque bolted to his prosthetic arm with the names of the 75th Regiment's fallen soldiers. That honor roll includes Specialist Christopher Gathercole, who died of the wound he suffered in the courtyard on May 26, 2008.

In 2011, Leroy Petry became only the second recipient of the Medal of Honor from the post-9/11 wars in Iraq and Afghanistan to accept the award in person. When asked of his feelings about the award, he quoted his son as summing them up best.

"They asked, 'How do you feel about your dad receiving the Medal of Honor and being at the White House?' He said, 'I'm pretty proud of my dad, but I'm happy that he saved two of his friends and they're still here.'"

Chapter 15

The Lone Defender

Army Sergeant Ryan M. Pitts

Wanat lay at the bottom of steeply terraced hillsides carved at the feet of soaring mountains in the remote Waygal Valley. The village boasted a large hotel, a mosque, and a bazaar where the villagers sold produce and handicrafts. In summer the days were hot and the nights surprisingly cool, good weather for travelers who found themselves in this remote corner of Nuristan Province.

In early July 2008, visitors to Wanat included forty-eight U.S. paratroopers from Chosen Company, 2nd Battalion, 503rd Infantry Regiment of the 173rd Airborne Brigade. Chosen Company and its Afghan partners arrived in Wanat under the cover of darkness and set up "Vehicle Patrol Base Kahler" inside a partially walled compound on the outskirts of town. Their mission was to extend the Afghan government's authority and counter insurgent activity in the isolated region.

U.S. operations in Afghanistan had reached a dangerous inflection point by 2008. For years the war in Iraq had siphoned off the bulk of U.S. forces and equipment, and Taliban and Al Qaeda forces that had been routed earlier in the war had long since regrouped in sanctuaries in the wild tribal areas of nearby Pakistan.

The harrowing experiences of the 173rd Airborne during its yearlong deployment reflected that shift in the balance of power. In August 2007, Chosen Company had barely repelled a major Taliban attack on Combat Outpost Ranch. In October

they engaged in fierce fighting as part of Operation Rock Avalanche in the nearby Korengal Valley. By the summer of 2008,
their task force found its "Sky Soldiers" scattered over eighteen
satellite bases in some of the most inhospitable mountain terrain on earth, without the heavy equipment needed to fortify
their positions and low on the critical aerial surveillance necessary to track enemy movements.

A few days into the Wanat deployment, Sergeant Ryan Pitts
and eight other paratroopers found themselves providing overwatch of the village from Observation Post Topside, little more
than a ring of sandbags and concertina wire a hundred meters
or so up the terraced hillside. Ever since kindergarten the young
New Englander from Nashua, New Hampshire, had dreamed
of becoming a soldier. In 2003, at the age of just seventeen,
Pitts had made the dream reality by enlisting in the Army on
a delayed entry program, knowing full well that he was signing up for war. In 2008 he was just twenty-two years old, and
already on his second combat deployment to Afghanistan.

The nine-member team at Topside acted as the base camp
commander's eyes and ears, and their mission was to alert
him to any unusual activity around Wanat. As a forward
observer, Pitts's job was to serve as the unit's link to indirect
fire from mortar positions, and to identify targets for attack
aircraft in case they were needed. Mostly what Pitts observed
was the intense curiosity of the Afghan villagers. Groups of

men sitting along the rock walls near the bazaar and having tea on the patio beside the hotel seemed intently focused on what their new neighbors were doing. One man even climbed a tree on the hillside near Topside to get a better look over the sandbags, until Pitts and the others motioned for him to climb down and move on. The American soldiers were definitely being watched.

Shortly before dawn on July 13, U.S. and Afghan soldiers at Vehicle Patrol Base Kahler beside the village were mustering for a "stand to" formation, preparing to conduct patrols and further fortify their vulnerable position. Looking down from his perch on Topside, Pitts noticed that the village was eerily quiet. Usually by that time Afghan villagers were already lighting cooking fires and walking out to work the fields. On this morning Wanat looked like a ghost town.

Over the radio, the soldier manning the infrared target acquisition scope for a TOW missile system reported seeing a suspicious group of Afghan men walking along the hillside some fifteen hundred meters above town. Already on edge because of the unnatural quiet, Sergeant Pitts immediately began plotting a possible mortar strike. There was little chance that the Afghan men were civilians out for a stroll on the mountainside at that time of the morning.

A staccato burst of machine-gun fire echoed in the valley, causing U.S. troops to scatter for cover. Heads swiveled toward a two-story building at the north end of town where the fire originated. As if on cue, the entire valley erupted with bright muzzle flashes and the smoky contrails of rocket-propelled grenades. Explosions rent the early morning air and automatic weapons fire crackled from the hotel, the bazaar, and even the mosque. The initial volley concentrated on the U.S. mortar positions and on the armored Humvee that carried the TOW system, the most effective and long-range U.S. weapon. The TOW vehicle quickly burst into flame, scattering missiles across the base that soldiers picked up with their bare hands to try and secure them. This was no hit-and-run attack by a ragtag band of mountain insurgents. It was a coordinated and synchronized attack by an estimated two hundred combat-seasoned Taliban fighters.

Observation Post Topside took a direct hit from multiple rocket-propelled grenades that detonated inside its perimeter. Hand grenades were tossed over the sandbags from a brush-filled creekbed just outside the concertina wire, exploding in their midst. Within minutes all nine U.S. paratroopers at Topside were wounded, some of them severely.

Sergeant Ryan Pitts crouched behind the sandbags, trying in vain to cover up and hoping for an end to a string of explosions that seemed to last forever. In a brief lull he tried to shake it off and get his bearings. Shrapnel had shredded both of his legs and his left arm. A wound on his inner thigh bled so heavily that he feared a major artillery was severed. He stared at his feet and silently ordered them to move so he could stand up and get into the fight. *Nothing.*

Pitts crawled across the fighting position to the south end that had been designated a casualty collection point. He was bleeding badly, but when he reached Sergeant Matthew

Gobble the soldier was also wounded and too disoriented to help. Specialist Jason Bogar was returning fire from behind the sandbags. Bogar took one look at Pitts and stopped firing long enough to put a tourniquet on Pitts's right leg above the thigh wound. Then he picked his M4 rifle back up and started firing again.

In the chaos, Specialist Tyler Stafford crawled over, also bleeding from multiple wounds. He told Pitts that Specialists Matthew Phillips and Gunnar Zwilling had both been killed in the initial explosions. Stafford said he thought they had been killed by insurgents who were throwing hand grenades into the observation post from the nearby creekbed.

Pitts felt the anger rise. He got that the insurgents really wanted to kill them all, but some of the Americans soldiers were still alive, and they were getting really pissed off. And then Pitts thought about what Stafford had said. *Well, if they can throw hand grenades, so can we.*

With automatic weapons fire raking their position and whistling overhead, Pitts crawled back to the northern part of the fighting position where they kept the grenades. The insurgents were so close that he could hear their voices just outside the wire. He picked up a grenade and pulled the pin, and then he held the live explosive in his hand—cooking off the fuse for one second, and then another, and another still—before finally hurling it toward the voices so that the insurgents would have no time to throw it back. After feeling the satisfying explosion, Pitts picked up another grenade and repeated the risky motion. And then he picked up another.

Needing to conserve their last hand grenades, Pitts grabbed an M240 machine gun lying nearby. He was still unable to stand on shredded legs, so he fired over the waist-high wall of sandbags, blindly at first to suppress enemy incoming, then propped himself on his knees to lay down more accurate fire. In the midst of the desperate fight he was startled to see the head of First Lieutenant Jonathan Brostrom pop up over the sandbags. Then Brostrom and Specialist Jason Hovater jumped into their post and took up fighting positions. That Brostrum and Hovater were willing and able to maneuver from base camp Kahler to Topside under heavy enemy fire with scant cover was little short of miraculous. But Pitts wasn't surprised. Lieutenant Brostrom was a natural leader and a fighter, and it was just like him to try and reinforce his wounded men in the heat of battle, whatever the risks. That's why they all loved him.

Pitts gave Lieutenant Brostrom a quick situation report, then surrendered his machine gun to Specialist Pruitt Rainey, giving them all the ammo he could grab. Rainey handed Pitts an M4 rifle with a 203 grenade launcher attached. As Brostrom, Hovater, Rainey, and Bogar took up fighting positions and fired their weapons furiously to hold the defensive perimeter of Topside and keep it from being overrun, Pitts manned the radio and began to call in indirect fire requests to base camp.

At one point there was a lull in the firing, and Pitts looked around the suddenly quiet observation post. There didn't seem to be any defensive fire coming out of their position. He couldn't call out and risk alerting the enemy to his position and situation, so he once again crawled quietly to the south-ernmost edge of the perimeter. He saw only the bodies of dead U.S. soldiers. He crawled over to the "crow's nest" observation position and found no one there. As he crawled painfully back to the northern edge of the post, the realization struck him like a death sentence: He was badly hurt and alone.

Reaching for the radio mic, Pitts contacted "Chosen 6," Captain Matthew Meyer, his commander down at Vehicle Patrol Base Kahler. The situation there was also dire. The other wounded defenders at Topside had retreated to a casu-alty collection point at the main base after their callout for survivors went unanswered. The troops sent to reinforce Top-side, Lieutenant Brostrom and Specialist Hovater, had been killed defending the position, along with Specialists Bogar and Rainey. Now Pitts was badly wounded and alone and asking for more reinforcements they didn't have, the voices of enemy fighters so close that Meyer could hear them over Pitts's radio.

"Everyone is dead or gone from the OP, and we need help up here," Pitts whispered to his commander over the radio.

"I don't have anybody to send," Meyer told him.

"Roger. Well, either you send more people or this place falls," said Ryan Pitts, signing off and laying down his radio. There wasn't anything else to talk about. He even agreed with Meyer's decision. There was nothing else that could be done. Pitts's time was up, and the young soldier made his peace with that reality.

He could still hear the voices of the insurgents all around

the perimeter of Topside. Some sounded like they were already inside the wire. As he bled out, his one final wish was to kill as many of them as possible before he died. He pulled the pin, cooked off the fuse, and hurled his last grenade. He grabbed the grenade launcher and fired it nearly straight up into the sky so that the grenade would tumble back down on the enemy fighters just on the other side of the sandbags. An Afghan insurgent leapt up on top of the barrier nearby, firing down as Pitts braced for the end.

But paratroopers of the 173rd Airborne Brigade leave no man behind on the battlefield. Fire from an unexpected direction drove the insurgent back, and a reinforcement team of four Chosen Company soldiers jumped over the sandbagged wall of Topside. Staff Sergeant Sean Samaroo, Sergeant Israel Garcia, and Specialist Michael Denton immediately took up firing positions to drive the insurgents back, as Specialist Jacob Sones worked to stabilize Pitts, who was weakened by blood loss and multiple concussions.

As he fought for consciousness and watched his friends take charge, Ryan Pitts had one overwhelming thought.

"Thank God I'm not alone."

Another volley of rocket-propelled grenades slammed into Observation Post Topside, the explosions hurling chunks of molten shrapnel. All four soldiers in the reinforcement team were hit. Despite their wounds, three of the soldiers continued to return fire and keep the insurgents from overrunning the position. Ryan Pitts looked around and saw that Sergeant Garcia was hit badly, and he crawled over to his friend and held his hand. Garcia was an immigrant from Mexico and there was no more proud American soldier. He was on his third combat tour defending his adopted country.

As he lay dying, Israel Garcia asked Pitts to tell his wife and mother that he loved them.

Time is a fungible concept in the crucible of battle. Adrenaline can compress and warp it, while pain, grief, and weariness can stretch it out to infinity. It may have been minutes or it may have been longer, but soon the Apache gunships arrived and Ryan Pitts was back working the radio, bringing their devastating firepower "danger close" and just yards away to keep Topside from being overrun. Eventually the Taliban fighters fell back.

Nine U.S. soldiers fell in the Battle of Wanat, one of the fiercest of the long Afghan War. The honor roll includes Specialist Sergio Abad, an expectant father whose dream of having a beautiful baby girl later came true; Corporal Jonathan Ayers, a motorcycle-loving athlete who took a direct hit in the helmet but kept on fighting; Corporal Jason Bogar, a gifted photographer whose pictures of the Afghan people captivated the company; First Lieutenant Jonathan Brostrom, a father who loved surfing with his son and who braved withering enemy fire to come to the aid of his wounded men; Sergeant Israel Garcia, the Mexican immigrant who died with the name of his beloved wife, Lesly, on his lips; Corporal Jason

Hovater, a cut-up whose jokes belied a deep faith; Corporal Matthew Phillips, an adventurous spirit and husband who always seemed to have a smile on his face; Corporal Pruitt Rainey, a big man with a big heart and a wicked good poker player; and Corporal Gunnar Zwilling, the guitar-playing "little brother" of the unit who along with the others died far too young so that Chosen Company could hold its ground in the Battle of Wanat.

The last thing Sergeant Ryan Pitts remembered about the battle was lying at the casualty collection point as fellow soldiers popped smoke canisters for concealment, and then seeing the medivac helicopter come swooping improbably into the still hot landing zone, the pilots and aircrew risking their lives to bring their brothers in arms to safety. The sight evoked the valor and professionalism that had surrounded him that terrible day, and Pitts thought it was the most incredible thing he ever saw.

Chapter 16

———★———

The Battle of Ganjgal

Army Captain William D. Swenson

Marine Corps Corporal
Dakota L. Meyer

They were about as different as two Americans fighting on the same side could be. One was a thirty-year-old Army captain, the laid-back son of two college professors from Seattle who had once aspired to a job in the diplomatic corps. The other was a decidedly undiplomatic twenty-one-year-old Marine corporal and farm kid from small-town Kentucky who found a home in the Corps as a sniper and gunner.

Yet the paths of William Swenson and Dakota Meyer intersected fatefully on September 8, 2009, in Afghanistan's remote Ganjgal Valley. Their actions that day would lead to both being awarded the Medal of Honor, only the second time in nearly half a century that the nation's highest award for valor was presented to two survivors of the same battle.

As Dakota Meyer details in his harrowing book-length memoir *Into the Fire*, he first crossed paths with Swenson at a mission briefing for Operation Buri Booza, or "Dancing Goat II," an outreach to elders in the mountain village of Ganjgal. For ten months Swenson had advised a local Afghan Border Police unit, while Meyer was part of a Marine Corps Embedded Training Team mentoring elements of the Afghan National Army. After eight years of fighting, the United States was eager to shift security responsibilities to local Afghan forces, and Dancing Goat was part of a series of trial runs to test their readiness to take the lead in defending their own country.

Meyer was glad to see the quiet Army captain with the shock of long hair sitting in the briefing room. Swenson was on his third combat tour, and after logging over a hundred leadership engagements with the mountain clans he had a Lawrence of Arabia–type reputation for working well with the local tribes. Once a Marine patrol stopping by a border police chief's compound in a remote valley had been surprised to greet a beardless American wearing the flowing robes and flat *pakol* hat of the Afghan tribesmen. Swenson had been invited to a local wedding and had stayed in the mountains for a week as the chief's guest.

As Dakota Meyer recounts in his book, he was most interested in Captain Swenson's reputation for calling in indirect artillery and mortar fire with deadly accuracy, a prized and difficult skill in the mountains. Because his four-man "Team Monti" would be at the front of the convoy for Dancing Goat, Meyer planned to introduce himself to Swenson after the briefing to compare preset target coordinates.

But the briefer informed them that there would be no convoy. The photomap in the briefing room showed the village of Ganjgal as two small hamlets of sturdy cement and stone compounds clinging to steeply terraced hillsides at the end of a box canyon. The hamlets were separated by a rutted gravel wash formed by mountain streams when the snows melted. There was only one way in and out of the valley on a narrow, ungraded trail. Because of concerns about improvised explosive devices and a desire not to telegraph their early morning approach, the mission leaders planned for the roughly one hundred U.S. and Afghan troops and police to exit their vehicles at a predetermined rally point and walk the final stretch to the village.

"We're walking in?" Meyer asked the briefer incredulously. Their greatest protection was armored Humvees armed with fearsome .50 caliber machine guns and grenade launchers. "We're not taking our gun trucks?"

"No. We're going in at dawn," said First Lieutenant Ademola Fabayo, a member of the command team for the operation, who was not interested in pushback from a twenty-one-year-old corporal. "The noise of trucks would alert them. I don't want to lose the element of surprise."

The briefer was unaware of an intelligence report that came into the tactical operations center that evening from a Special Forces observation team. A force of more than thirty Taliban fighters had been spotted moving from Pakistan through the mountain pass above Ganjgal, and the video feed from a U.S. drone showed other groups of fighters falling in on known insurgent safe houses and moving on the hillsides above the village. One of the Special Forces commandos attached a note to the intelligence report that amounted to a flashing warning signal: "Their movement is too organized to be locals; they have a point man, security element, and overwatch. Locals do not move like this. They are utilizing terrain, stopping under cover, and hesitating at all open areas."

During the Soviet Red Army's long, bloody war in Afghanistan, the valley of Ganjgal Gar served as a major supply artery between sanctuaries in nearby Pakistan and the Afghan

interior, with Ganjgal village as key way station for mujahedeen fighters. Tragically, intelligence indicating that the infiltration route was once again teeming with insurgents never
reached the commanders of Dancing Goat II. The Americans
and their Afghan partners were walking into a trap.

Shortly before dawn the convoy of open-backed Ford Ranger
pickup trucks and four U.S. armored Humvees reached the
jumping-off point, and the troops disembarked. At the last
moment Corporal Meyer had been informed that he was being
replaced on the four-man Team Monti by Gunnery Sergeant
Edwin Johnson, and he was crestfallen. The rest of the Embedded Training Team—Lieutenant Michael Johnson, Staff Sergeant Aaron Kenefick, and Navy corpsman James Layton—all
argued against the last-minute switch, having come to trust
Meyer both as a gunner and field tactician, with a cool head
under fire. Their protests fell on deaf ears. Meyer was con-
vinced that the change resulted from his being viewed as too
headstrong and outspoken by higher headquarters, and Lieutenant Johnson agreed.

"Meyer, it's your bad," Johnson told him as recounted in
Into the Fire. "If you learned to kiss ass, or at least not kick
people in the ass, you'd be coming with us. But no, that's not
your style."

Ordered to stay behind and guard the trucks, Meyer promised Lieutenant Johnson that if things got hairy, he would drive

in with an armored Humvee and pull the team out. "Radio your coordinates and get down to the wash. Fucking climb in and we'll haul ass back to the main body."

Team Monti and an Afghan Army platoon set out at the head of the long column of troops. Just behind them was the tactical command party consisting of Major Kevin Williams, Lieutenant Fabayo, First Sergeant Christopher Garza, and Afghan major Tallib, along with embedded reporter Jonathan Landay. They were followed by Captain Swenson and his trusted noncommissioned officer Sergeant Ken Westbrook, an "Army of two," as Swenson sometimes joked. As they set out, the lights of Ganjgal village twinkled in the dark roughly a mile to the east.

Dakota Meyer was sitting on the hood of his Humvee talking with Staff Sergeant Juan Rodriguez-Chavez, bitching about being left behind to babysit the vehicles. Rodriguez-Chavez had grown up on a ranch in Mexico and immigrated to Texas as a young teenager. A proud husband and father of two daughters, the man they called "Hot Rod" talked fondly of roping cows in rodeos and living the ranch life. He and Meyer got along famously.

As the two young Marines were talking, the lights in Ganjgal village were suddenly extinguished, as if someone had flicked a circuit breaker. Warnings to keep a lookout for "dushmen," or Taliban fighters, sounded on the adviser radio net, and some of the Afghan border police slowed their walking and then drifted back to the rear of the column. Soon Meyer and Rodriguez-Chavez heard gravel crunching on the trail. A crowd of men, women, and children fleeing the village hurried by the vehicles, unwilling to even stop long enough to return their greeting. Corporal Dakota Meyer knew then what was about to go down, but still the column of American and Afghan troops trudged deeper into the valley.

As dawn broke, Lieutenant Johnson and the rest of Team Monti entered the outskirts of South Ganjgal, seeking the house of a village elder and local imam. On the series of terraces below, each level supported by a stone retaining wall, the long column of troops and police was spread out, with rear elements still crossing the open wash on the valley floor. With the sun behind the multiple fighting positions the Taliban had established inside the village and in unseen trenches along the surrounding ridgelines, Qari Zia Ur-Rahman, a veteran fighter and head of the organization in Kunar Province, sprang his trap.

A rocket-propelled grenade fired at close range exploded near Team Monti, initiating the ambush. Instantly machine-gun and automatic weapons fire erupted from the stone houses throughout the village and from the surrounding hillsides. The impacts stitched nearby walls and ricocheted off the ground, and Lieutenant Johnson and his three teammates ducked inside the courtyard of a walled house. They were quickly pinned down by intense gunfire from the surrounding buildings. The rest of the column scrambled for cover behind the terrace walls. The fearsome, pile-driving report of a large Russian antiaircraft gun echoed in the valley.

Crouching behind a stone wall, Captain Swenson immediately did what he did best: call in accurate suppressive fire from U.S. artillery and mortar positions, while requesting immediate air support. Between radio calls he pointed out targets for Lieutenant Fabayo to engage with his M4 rifle. On the terrace behind, Major Williams and Sergeant Garza returned fire, but it was like spitting into a hailstorm. Swenson saw Taliban fighters swarm out of trenches and from behind boulders on the high ground to the east, attempting to flank their positions. *They're all over the place*, Swenson thought. *I may not make it out of here.*

"This is Highlander 6!" he shouted over the deafening sounds of battle, giving predetermined targeting coordinates. "Forward line of troops pinned down. Heavy enemy fire. Request immediate suppression!"

Not for the last time that morning, Swenson's request for indirect suppressive fire and smoke to extract Team Monti was denied or met with a barrage of unanswerable questions: You are too close to the village to risk civilian casualties. What is the disposition of all friendly forces? Has everyone been accounted for? According to *Into the Fire*, in the first desperate hour in the Battle of Ganjgal, the tactical operations center back at Forward Operating Base Joyce fired only twenty-one artillery shells, far too few to be effective. Air support also failed to arrive after having earlier been diverted to what was considered a higher-priority operation.

Emboldened by the ineffective artillery fire and lack of air support, Taliban fighters began streaming down the ridgelines to flank the American and Afghan Army troops pinned down behind the terrace walls. Friendly wounded began piling up. Major Williams was shot in the arm, and Sergeant Garza's eardrums were ruptured by the blast of a rocket-propelled grenade.

Taking charge, Captain Swenson realized they had to retreat from the terraced hillside or be surrounded and killed. He and Lieutenant Fabayo provided covering fire for the group as it bounded over open ground and then jumped down a terrace wall. Before he could join them, Swenson heard over the radio that his friend Sergeant Ken Westbrook had been shot in the neck and lay where he fell in the open.

Swenson fired and maneuvered toward Westbrook with three Afghan Army soldiers. Before he could reach his friend two of the Afghan soldiers were cut down by enemy fire and killed, and the other was wounded. Lieutenant Fabayo, Sergeant Garza, and embedded reporter Jonathan Landay broke cover and ran into the open under fire to drag Westbrook to cover behind a terrace wall. Swenson sprinted across the final fifty meters of open ground to reach Westbrook and help render first aid.

By this time Taliban fighters had closed to within twenty or so yards of the group, ready for the kill. Four Taliban rounded a nearby corner of a retaining wall and Lieutenant Fabayo shot the lead man dead. The other three quickly ducked back behind cover. The Americans and their Afghan partners were on the verge of being overrun.

Swenson's Afghan interpreter was monitoring the police radio net when a Taliban commander broke in. "The Russians made the same mistake coming here," he taunted the Americans and their Afghan partners. "The elders invited you in; I decide if you leave. You must surrender."

Captain William Swenson stopped treating Westbrook for a moment to prepare his answer. He pulled the pin on a grenade and hurled it toward the excited voices of the nearby Taliban fighters. The explosion was followed by a moment of silence, and then the Afghan Army and American troops nearby rallied and laid down a barrage of fire that momentarily drove the Taliban back outside of grenade range.

Roughly ninety minutes into the firefight, two OH-58 Kiowa scout helicopters swooped into the valley. Swenson stopped treating Westbrook long enough to man the radio and direct them onto the encircling enemy. The suppressive fire provided a brief opportunity, and Swenson ordered everyone to pull back two hundred meters to a casualty collection point. Swenson, Fabayo, and the embedded reporter, Landay, alternately helped to carry a barely conscious Westbrook, with Major Williams and Sergeant Garza carrying gear and returning fire as the group stumbled forward, bounding down the terraces and across a wide expanse of broken ground in the wash. Twice the group of walking wounded had to stop and duck for cover as machine-gun fire and rocket-propelled grenades impacted close by.

At the casualty collection point, Swenson helped load Westbrook into a medivac helicopter. In the whipping rotor wash and roar of the helicopter blades, Swenson leaned down and kissed his wounded friend on the head. A video from a camera inside the helicopter captured the tender goodbye, revealing in a rare glimpse the love that sustains troops through the horrors of combat. It was the last time that William Swenson saw the other half of his "Army of two" alive.

Before the UH-60 medivac helicopter even cleared the valley ridge, Captain Swenson and Lieutenant Fabayo commandeered an unarmored Ford Ranger pickup and drove back into the kill zone to try and evacuate more wounded, and to search for the missing Team Monti. With bullets soon kicking up geysers and slamming into the pickup truck as it bounced through the wash, their chances of survival were slim.

"By that time it didn't matter," Fabayo would later say. "We weren't going to leave any soldiers behind."

Staff Sergeant Juan Rodriguez-Chavez steered the bouncing Humvee through the rocky wash, bullets pinging off the armor, as Corporal Dakota Meyer stood in the turret and blasted away with the .50 caliber machine gun. Taliban fighters up ahead were sprinting directly across their path, and firing from unseen trenches and gullies. Hot Rod and Dakota had driven right into the rear of the kill sack that the enemy zipped tight behind the formation, trapping the U.S. and Afghan Army troops inside. Five or six Afghan Army troops crouching behind a terrace wall some hundred yards away leapt to their feet and ran toward the U.S. Humvee in hopes of evacuation. One by one they were all shot as they ran, pitching forward.

Meyer was frozen a moment by the sight. There were bodies of the dead and wounded scattered everywhere like a scene from a war movie. Then he caught a glimpse of movement and turned to see a Taliban fighter jump out of a ditch and sprint toward the rear of the truck. Meyer swiveled the big machine gun and cut the fighter down. Rod was yelling something, and Meyer saw another Taliban trying to open the right door. Unable to point the barrel of the mounted .50 caliber that low, he grabbed his M4 rifle by instinct and shot the man in the neck and head. Feeling as well as hearing the hum of a bullet that nearly grazed his cheek and others that ricocheted inside the turret, Meyer looked down to see blood from a wound on his arm.

Up ahead another Taliban ran to the front of the truck, firing his AK-47 from the hip. Hot Rod gunned the engine and ran him over. Dakota Meyer had to force himself not to duck down into the cover of the armored Humvee to escape the enemy bullets, knowing that they would be swarmed. He had zero doubt that he was going to die.

Four times Meyer had requested permission from the tactical operations center to come to the aid of Team Monti and the rest of the formation, and each time the request was denied. Local command-and-control had broken down in the chaos of battle, and even the quick reaction force was hesitant to drive straight into an ambush where the enemy commanded the heights. Finally Meyer had heard his boss, Lieutenant Johnson from Team Monti, come onto the radio net, stating matter-of-factly that his team was under intense fire and surrounded, and asking for smoke rounds to conceal their retreat from Ganjgal. The request was denied by the tactical operations center because their position was deemed too close to "civilian" structures.

"Too close to the village! If you don't give me these rounds right now I'm gonna die!" Johnson replied on the radio, according to Meyer's account.

That settled the matter for Meyer and Rodriguez-Chavez, who disobeyed a direct order and drove into the kill zone to try and reach Team Monti. By the time they made it into the wash they ran across a group of badly wounded Afghan soldiers. Meyer helped load five of the bloodied soldiers into the truck and then evacuated them back to the casualty collection point. For a second time they drove back into the ambush kill zone and picked up wounded Afghan soldiers until Meyer's gun jammed. They returned to the casualty collection point to drop off the wounded Afghans and exchange guns. Then Meyer and Rodriguez-Chavez entered the kill zone for a third time, only to be nearly swarmed by Taliban fighters.

After fighting through to the wash once again, they came across a group of U.S. soldiers who were desperately trying to escape the ambush. Hot Rod maneuvered the Humvee so that it was between the American troops and the line of enemy fire from the nearest terrace, and Meyer laid down suppressive fire as they provided cover for the group to escape.

By midmorning Captain Swenson and Rodriguez-Chavez were back at the rally point, where they commandeered a fresh Humvee and picked up Dakota Meyer to once again search for Team Monti. Lieutenant Fabayo was in the turret manning the .50 caliber, and their Afghan interpreter, Hafez, was in the back with Meyer. Swenson was riding shotgun in the command seat talking over the radio to two OH-58 Kiowa scout helicopters that were swooping dangerously low over the housing compounds of Ganjgal trying to locate Team Monti.

Once again the Americans were forced to stop in order to render aid to wounded Afghan Army soldiers and to help them move out of the line of fire or into Afghan Army pickup trucks that were bringing up the rear. As mentors to the Afghan forces, they couldn't let them just bleed to death without stopping to help.

With the highly maneuverable OH-58 Kiowas suppressing enemy fire with .50 caliber machine guns, the Humvee neared the outskirts of the village. They were all bloodied and beyond exhaustion, and worried about the missing team. Swenson had to pull rank to keep the headstrong Meyer from jumping out of the armored truck and searching the compounds by himself.

"I'm an Army captain, Corporal," Swenson told the young Marine. "I'm giving you a direct order. Stay in the damn truck. We're all here to find them. It's not just you."

Shortly afterward, the radio crackled with the news they all dreaded.

"Highlander, we've spotted five bodies," said the Kiowa pilot, using Swenson's call sign.

Dakota Meyer was the first to reach his team, who were clustered in a deep trench near the compound where they had been surrounded. Gunnery Sergeant Edwin Johnson lay on his back, unseeing eyes staring at the sky. Lieutenant Michael Johnson was also on his back with an entry wound in his right shoulder. "Doc" James Layton had fallen on top of his commander as if to cover him, his medical supplies scattered around and his face disfigured by point-blank gunshots. Staff Sergeant Aaron Kenefick was facedown, shot in the back of his head. The body of their Afghan interpreter also lay nearby.

The story told by their bodies was clear, and the absence of most of their gear and weapons confirmed the truth: While treating their wounded and waiting for the help that never came, Team Monti had been overrun and massacred.

The recovery team was still taking sporadic incoming fire. Sergeant Rodriguez-Chavez and Lieutenant Fabayo provided covering fire. Meyer, Swenson, and some of the Afghan Army troops silently loaded the bodies and remaining gear into the back of their trucks, and then set out on the long, lonely trip home.

As it turned out, Army captain William Swenson and Marine corporal Dakota Meyer had more in common than was apparent at first sight. In one of the deadliest and most intense small-arms battles of the Afghan War, both braved overwhelming odds and repeatedly ran through withering enemy gunfire to come to the aid of their brothers in arms, Afghan as well as American. Neither thought there was much of a choice in the matter. In the end, five Americans died in the Battle of Ganjgal, including the four members of Team Monti and Sergeant Westbrook, who later succumbed to his wounds. Ten Afghan troops were also killed, and there were seventeen coalition wounded.

"I didn't just lose four guys that day, I lost ten brothers, because the Afghans were just as close to me as any Marines I ever served with," Meyer later said in an interview on the Jocko Willink podcast. "The brotherhood I had with them is why I'm alive today."

When asked later, during an appearance at Loyola University, why he chose to repeatedly return to the fight and face likely death, Swenson thought for a moment and then insisted that it wasn't really a difficult decision. "Well, we were a team, and what seems like a bad idea now was the right thing to do then," he said, stressing that it was always devotion to the team that kept him going. "You have fellow service members who need your help, and that's your responsibility. You have to weight that decision against potential outcomes and what the consequences might be, and then you make a decision. In that case we made a decision to reenter the valley, because that's what we were called to do."

Captain William Swenson became the first Army officer since the Vietnam War to be awarded the Medal of Honor. At just twenty-one years old during the Battle of Ganjgal, Corporal Dakota Meyer was one of the youngest recipients of the Medal of Honor in recent decades. Their medals represented one of only a few times in nearly half a century that the nation's highest award for valor was presented to two survivors of the same battle.

Both William Swenson and Dakota Meyer also struggled with post-traumatic stress and the demons they brought home from Afghanistan and the Battle of Ganjgal. Both have spoken publicly about that struggle to reduce the stigma and inspire other service members troubled by the memories of war to seek professional help.

In Meyer's case his struggles with survival guilt over the failure to rescue his four friends on Team Monti nearly consumed him. In his book and subsequent interviews, he describes a dark, drunken night of the soul when he put a pistol to his head and pulled the trigger. He only survived by the grace of a loved one with enough foresight to secretly remove the ammunition from his Glock pistol.

"From that moment I put away the pistol, I knew that quitting wasn't right. Not that night. Not ever," said Meyer, who wears the names of his fallen teammates on two arm bracelets. "Any day I don't want to push on, I got four reasons right here—men who would switch with me on my worst day just to have one more day. So I'm not okay with letting their sacrifice go to waste."

Chapter 17

———✮———

Defending the Indefensible

Army Staff Sergeant Clinton L. Romesha

Army Specialist Ty M. Carter

There are place names with the power to strike dread in the psyches of those who fought there, map coordinates that carry an emotional gut punch and serve as shorthand for the myriad horrors of war: Ia Drang. Khe Sanh. Mogadishu. Fallujah. Sadr City. In America's longest war in Afghanistan, the real estate that most accurately captured the pitiless folly of the U.S. military's mountain campaign in the remote Hindu Kush was Combat Outpost Keating.

COP Keating was a collection of tin-roofed cement buildings and fighting positions roughly the size of a football field situated at the bottom of a gorge at the confluence of the Kushtowz and Landay Sin rivers. The base and the adjacent village of Kamdesh were surrounded on all sides by towering mountains. In October 2009, COP Keating was defended by fifty-three U.S. soldiers of Bravo Troop, 3rd Squadron, 61st Cavalry Regiment, 4th Brigade Combat Team, along with a small contingent of Afghan National Army troops.

The U.S. soldiers derisively called COP Keating a "fishbowl," because it made them feel like fish in a barrel. Enemy snipers and grenadiers targeted them so regularly from behind boulders and trees on the surrounding hillsides that the U.S. soldiers suited up in body armor just to venture outside or chance a walk to the latrine. After enough time at COP Keating, soldiers' faces were drawn from the constant stress, and their bodies were pasty white from lack of sunlight. In the roughly five months that Bravo Troop had occupied Keating they had been hit forty-seven times in what intelligence briefers considered harassing attacks. The tough mountain fighters who studied the reactions of U.S. troops to each attack knew them as probes.

When Staff Sergeant Clinton Romesha, known as Clint, first looked around COP Keating he was struck by the stunning beauty of the mountains and the frothing rivers at their base. Studying the steep hillsides overlooking the outpost, he also knew the outpost was a tactical nightmare. The first morning on Keating he thought, *I'm going to have the strongest neck muscles from looking up for an entire year.*

One of five siblings and the child of a Vietnam veteran, Romesha grew up in the small California town of Lake City, population a buck and change. One of his fondest memories was visiting his grandfather's small ranch in Vya, Nevada. Aury Smith was a World War II veteran who took his brother's place in the draft, and later landed on Normandy shortly after D-Day. Granddad's stories of "the greatest generation," and insistence that his grandkids had a responsibility to bring honor to the family name, made an impression on young Clint. Shortly after turning eighteen, Romesha enlisted in the Army as an M1 tank crewman, and later transitioned to reconnaissance scout, eventually serving two tours in Iraq.

★ ★ ★

Sunlight crowned the peaks surrounding Combat Outpost Keating at dawn of October 3, 2009. Staff Sergeant Clint Romesha awoke to the booming report of a Soviet B-10 recoilless rifle echoing in the fishbowl. Loud explosions and the metallic rattle of machine guns soon added to the cacophony. As he rolled out of bed and grabbed his gear, Romesha knew instinctively from the intensity of the incoming fire that this was not enemy harassment or probing, but the full-on enemy assault on COP Keating that Bravo Troop had long feared.

The most accurate and intense enemy fire was focused on their mortar positions and the armored Long Range Advanced Scout Surveillance (LRAS) vehicle in a fortified battle position at the southern end of the outpost near the front entry point, both key to the U.S. defenses. The estimated force of three hundred–plus Taliban fighters was well trained and led, and they picked their targets well.

In the initial chaos Romesha ran outside to LRAS 1, the armored Humvee guarding the tactical operations center. After confirming that Specialist Zachary Koppes was engaging enemy positions and trying to suppress the heavy incoming fire with the Mk 19 automatic grenade launcher, Romesha sprinted back to the barracks and grabbed an Mk 48 machine gun and drafted Specialist Justin Gregory as an assistant gunner.

Once outside, the pair ran at a crouch alongside the barracks building, but a barrage of RPG and machine-gun fire forced them to stop and take cover behind a generator. Romesha clearly saw a Taliban machine-gun team on high ground just to their west. He aimed the Mk 48 and walked the tracers across the position and destroyed it. Then he visually acquired another Taliban machine-gun team outside the front gate that was pouring fire onto his friends in the LRAS II Humvee at the south of the outpost. Romesha was so laser focused on destroying the second enemy machine-gun team that he never saw the Taliban fighter skirt along the hillside on his right flank. The rocket-propelled grenade scored a direct hit on the generator that they were using for cover, and the blast knocked Romesha on top of Gregory and peppered them both with shrapnel.

Specialist Ty Carter stumbled and zigzagged like a drunken man as explosive shock waves pushed him from side to side along a hundred-yard gauntlet of fire. The attack had come so suddenly that he barely had time to grab his body armor. For the second time that morning he was sprinting in the open carrying two sacks of ammunition for the LRAS II vehicle guarding the far southern flank of COP Keating, which was taking intense fire from multiple directions. Inside the Humvee, Sergeant Brad Larson, Staff Sergeant Justin Gallegos, and Specialist Stephan Mace had already burned through twelve hundred rounds of ammunition defending their vulnerable position.

Carter didn't need to be there. A former combat engineer from Spokane, Washington, he had been honorably discharged from the Marine Corps back in 2002, later enrolling in college at Los Medanos Community College in California and studying to become a biologist. Yet the birth of his first daughter filled him with a new sense of purpose, and Carter enlisted in the Army in 2008 to become a cavalry scout. Now it seemed unlikely he would ever see his baby girl again.

As Ty Carter approached the Humvee a series of well-aimed RPGs struck nearby, and he piled inside just in time to avoid being eviscerated. Sergeant Vernon Martin had also joined the team inside the crowded armored truck.

No sooner had they slammed the heavy door than another RPG blast rocked the carriage, and yet another scored a direct strike on their gun turret, destroying both of their crew-served machine guns and spraying razor-sharp shrapnel into Carter, Larson, and Martin. The enemy was closing in and the soldiers were unable to even risk cracking a bulletproof window to return fire as the Humvee rocked back and forth from successive blasts. It was only a matter of time before an RPG or some other armor-piercing weapon breached the vehicle's battered armor. They were caught in a death trap.

Sergeant Gallegos decided to try and make it back to the tactical operations center with Sergeant Martin and Specialist Mace. At the designated signal, Larson and Carter jumped out of the Humvee and laid down covering fire as their friends dashed back down the gauntlet. Before they had gone far an RPG landed nearby and the blast knocked the group to the ground, seriously wounding Mace. Sergeant Justin Gallegos staggered to his feet and stopped to help Mace, and was cut down by a burst of machine-gun fire from somewhere inside the wire. Sergeant Martin stumbled and fell, shot through the leg. He managed to crawl under the laundry trailer, where he would die of his wound. Grievously hurt, Specialist Mace crawled to low ground roughly thirty yards from the LRAS II Humvee. The soldiers had been picked off by a group of Taliban fighters that had breached the entry control point and were now inside COP Keating's perimeter.

Nearly out of ammunition and staggered by a shot to the helmet, Sergeant Larson shouted at Ty Carter.

"Get back in the vehicle!"

"Enemy in the wire! Enemy in the wire!"

The warning that every base commander in Afghanistan dreaded echoed through the tactical operations center (TOC) where Lieutenant Andrew Bundermann was trying to organize a last stand. Their Alamo was a collapsing perimeter around a small section of COP Keating that housed the TOC, a barracks building, and a medical aid station. In just over an hour, Bravo Troop had lost three soldiers killed in the fighting and seven more unaccounted for at the LRAS II vehicle. Electric power had gone down when the generator was hit, and some of the nearby outbuildings were burning out of control. The Afghan National Army soldiers guarding the east side of the base had abandoned their posts after suffering significant casualties. And now the enemy was spotted inside the wire.

Sergeant Clinton Romesha was just outside the TOC giving covering fire to Specialist Zach Koppes in the LRAS 1 gun truck. With his M4 running low on ammo, Romesha had grabbed a Dragunov sniper rifle from a wounded Afghan soldier, and was playing "peekaboo" with an enemy sniper. After neutralizing the enemy fighter, Romesha sought to link back up with his team and took cover behind the aid station. There he noticed three Taliban fighters crouching behind a Humvee inside their perimeter. The sight of the enemy moving through COP Keating and making themselves at home filled him with rage.

Romesha sighted the sniper rifle on a Taliban fighter who had just rested his rocket-propelled grenade launcher against the truck to adjust his headgear. He squeezed the trigger. Then he fired again, and again, ensuring that the intruders would never make it out of Keating alive.

Back in the TOC, Romesha confirmed that the Taliban were in fact moving inside the wire, and he asked for five volunteers to help secure the ammunition supply depot and the entry control point. Sergeant Matthew Miller, Private First Class Christopher Jones, and Specialists Josh Dannelley, Mark Dulaney, and Thomas Rassmussen all grabbed their weapons and volunteered without hesitation. With Romesha leading the way, the group moved in unison toward the ammunition point under heavy enemy fire and multiple RPG strikes. A group of Taliban fighters charged the barriers that ringed the building, and Romesha and the others threw fragmentation grenades to drive them back. In the melee, Josh Dannelley was shot in the arm, and Clinton Romesha helped evacuate him to the aid station.

Returning to the firefight, Romesha led the team toward the entry control point and the stranded LRAS II vehicle where he knew his best friend, Brad Larson, and the remaining members of his team were pinned down.

"I can't wait in this position any longer," Romesha radioed Lieutenant Bundermann. If they didn't secure the front gate, Romesha told his commander, the Taliban would surely start carting off the bodies of the American soldiers killed in action.

"Help me! *Please*. Help me!"

Specialist Stephan Mace was crawling on his elbows not thirty yards from the battered LRAS II Humvee, his body shattered by an RPG blast. His plaintive cries and the helpless look on his face were nearly driving Specialist Ty Carter out of his mind.

"Mace is right there. He's alive. I can get to him," Carter told Sergeant Larson, knowing in his heart that his chances of reaching his fellow soldier were slim to none. The bodies of dead American soldiers and Taliban fighters lay scattered all around the smoldering vehicle.

"No," Sergeant Larson told him. "You're no good to him dead."

The two soldiers were down to their last five or six rounds

of ammunition each, and their radio was dead. For all they knew, after countless hours of fighting they were the last soldiers still alive on COP Keating. If they could make it to nightfall they talked about trying to crawl to the nearby river and swim downstream without drowning, but neither really doubted that they were going to die.

Reinforcements finally arrived, but the hope they brought quickly turned to despair. A Humvee carrying Sergeant Joshua Hardt, Specialist Christopher Griffin, and Private Edward Faulkner Jr. pulled up near LRAS II and immediately attracted another withering barrage of rocket-propelled grenades. The explosions engulfed the vehicle, and a direct hit on the right passenger door wounded all three occupants. Hardt was the first to exit the vehicle, and he was immediately hit and killed by machine-gun fire. Griffin and Faulkner darted out and tried to make it across the open area back toward the command post, but Griffin was also shot and killed. Only Faulkner somehow made it to cover.

In the chaos, Ty Carter dashed to an abandoned Humvee nearby and secured ammunition and a grenade launcher before crawling back to Larson and LRAS II. They reloaded their M4 rifles and exited the Humvee to engage the swarming Taliban fighters. Carter killed a two-man RPG team, and then two more Taliban fighters just outside the wire. Their desperate defense was the only thing keeping the vulnerable southern flank of COP Keating from being completely overrun.

With Sergeant Larson laying down cover fire, Carter was given permission to try to reach Specialist Mace. Stephan Mace was in awful shape, bleeding from the abdomen, his leg blown all to hell. Carter tied a tourniquet around his leg, then checked Gallegos's body to confirm he was dead. After conferring with Larson, Carter made another mad dash to Mace under heavy fire and personally carried the wounded soldier to the LRAS II Humvee. As he laid Mace in the front passenger seat of the damaged Humvee, Carter gasped for breath, his lungs burning from the sulfer in the air from constant RPG strikes.

Running low on ammunition and with Mace in dire need of medical care, Carter decided to try and make it back to the tactical operations center. Once again Larson exited the Humvee and laid down suppressive fire while Carter took off, only to nearly stumble across the squad radio that Sergeant Gallegos had apparently dropped when he was hit. Carter tested it, heard blessed radio traffic, and sprinted back to Larson and Mace in the LRAS Humvee.

Nearby, Sergeant Romesha and his fire team were fighting furiously from a building next to the entry control point. The Taliban had captured the Afghan National Police checkpoint just in front of the control point, and the two sides were exchanging fire at nearly point-blank range. Close air support finally arrived and Romesha called out grid points on his radio. Soon bombs and mortars slammed down on Taliban positions, the deafening explosions killing an estimated thirty insurgents near the gate.

When Romesha heard on the radio that his friend Brad Larson was still alive but pinned down with an urgent casualty, he maneuvered his team to provide supporting fire for their evacuation. The command post also vectored in close air support that suppressed enemy fire positions on the hillsides nearby. With the enemy fire momentarily suppressed, Ty Carter and Brad Larson lay Stephan Mace on a stretcher, and together they carried him the roughly one hundred yards back to the aid station as they dodged sniper and machine-gun fire down the gauntlet. As they reached the aid station and medics began immediately giving Mace buddy-to-buddy blood transfusions, Ty Carter dropped to his knees in exhaustion.

The remaining defenders of COP Keating had been fighting for more than ten hours, and the outpost was a smoldering ruin. Bodies lay scattered across the base and the ground was littered with shell casings. All of the buildings were pockmarked with impact craters, and many were burning uncontrollably. And still the fighting continued.

When the fire spread to a tree next to the aid station and command center, Ty Carter once again exposed himself to enemy fire to cut it down with a chainsaw. Clinton Romesha led his team back to LRAS II to recover the bodies of the three American soldiers who died there, risking their lives so that the fallen were not desecrated by the enemy.

Only at nightfall did reinforcements with a quick reaction force finally reach COP Keating, and the defenders finally let their guard down enough to confront their loss. Twenty-two U.S. soldiers had been wounded, and seven of their friends had already died in the fighting: Justin T. Gallegos, Christopher Griffin, Kevin C. Thomson, Michael P. Scusa, Vernon W. Martin, Joshua J. Kirk, and Joshua M. Hardt.

Before that awful day was over, word reached the defenders that Specialist Stephan Mace had also died in surgery, despite all of their efforts to save him. The mood at COP Keating that night and in the days that followed was "absolutely terrible, because that's when the emotions hit," Ty Carter would later recall. "One of the things that kept me going was thinking that Larson and I were able to save Mace, and to hear that he died—I was destroyed."

The Battle for COP Keating was a further inflection point in the Afghan War. An Army investigation would later conclude that the outpost was "tactically indefensible" and of no real strategic value. Three days after the battle the U.S. military bombed Keating into oblivion, and began consolidating U.S. forces onto larger, more defensible bases and abandoning many of the small outposts situated in remote, hard-to-reach valleys in the Hindu Kush.

The American defenders of COP Keating constitute one of the most decorated units of the post-9/11 wars, with twenty-seven Purple Hearts, thirty-seven Army Commendation Medals with "V" devices to denote heroism, three Bronze Stars, eighteen Bronze Stars with "V" devices, and nine Silver Stars. Staff Sergeant Clinton Romesha and Specialist Ty Carter both received the Medal of Honor, the nation's highest award for valor, for their actions that day "above and beyond the call of duty."

Both Clint Romesha and Ty Carter were also haunted by what they witnessed on October 3, 2009, and have been open about the post-traumatic stress that has stalked the defenders of COP Keating. Private Ed Faulkner Jr. would fall prey to those demons, later reportedly suffering a mental breakdown and dying of an accidental overdose.

Post-traumatic stress "is very real, it's not a disorder. It's actually just a natural part of being human, because something bad happened," Carter said in a Military.com interview, recalling his bouts with flashbacks, nightmares, and nearly crippling anxiety. "So for people who feel embarrassed by it, it's because of the myths that are associated with it. I was totally believing the myths until it happened to me, and now I'm hoping that I can help people through what I have to say, and what I've experienced. To help them go seek help. Or else we're going to have more soldiers out there who self-medicate and end up taking their own lives."

Chapter 18

——☆——

An Indomitable Spirit

Marine Corps Lance Corporal
William "Kyle" Carpenter

K yle Carpenter stands on a hill under a gray sky and watches a funeral on the field below. There are no friends or family in attendance, not even a tombstone to mark the site. Just a lone pastor holding a Bible and looking into a freshly dug grave. Kyle wonders why he's even there when a terrifying realization overwhelms him: He's watching his own funeral and no one has bothered to come pay their respects. The Marine brothers he left behind in Afghanistan haven't forgiven him for leaving, and refused to even show up and say goodbye. He tries to yell but no sound escapes his lips. He is paralyzed as tears stream down his face.

As he recounts in his inspiring book, *You Are Worth It: Building a Life Worth Fighting For*, Carpenter awoke from that drug-induced nightmare to find himself at the National Naval Medical Center in Bethesda, Maryland, still tethered by tubes and wires to an operating room worth of equipment. On arrival in November 2010, he had spent five weeks in a medically induced coma. He still couldn't feel his face or lift his arms, and there didn't seem to be teeth in his mouth. He had lost an eye. Given the extent of his injuries, it was a miracle that he was even alive: Carpenter had gone into cardiac arrest and flatlined three times. Each time doctors had somehow brought him back to life.

As Carpenter recalls in his stirring book, the grenade blast had fractured his right arm in thirty places, and he was in danger of losing it. Much of his jaw had been blown away, and he had a skull fracture. He had shrapnel wounds from head to foot that had to be washed and re-dressed every forty-eight hours to stave off a potentially fatal infection. He was under a scalpel every second or third day as the surgeons at the medical center tried to stitch and fuse his flesh and bone back together. And the drug-induced hallucinations were so real that for all Kyle Carpenter knew the nightmare of witnessing his own funeral was a premonition.

Marine lance corporal Kyle Carpenter was part of a huge influx of Marines and soldiers who were flooding the polytrauma wards of U.S. military hospitals as the Defense Department surged forces to Afghanistan in 2009–10 to stave off a Taliban victory. Afghanistan had become a war of dismounted infantry, and troops were sustaining massive injuries from absorbing blasts, including multiple amputations, traumatic brain injury, severe burns, and the emotional toll and scars left in the wake of such catastrophic wounds.

The good news was that more American troops were surviving battlefield wounds in Afghanistan and Iraq than had their counterparts in any previous conflicts, including Somalia in 1992, the Persian Gulf War in 1991, or Vietnam in the 1960s and 1970s. For every death in Iraq and Afghanistan, 16 troops were wounded, compared with 2.4 wounded for every fatality in Vietnam.

In his book *Broken Bodies, Shattered Minds: A Medical Odyssey from Vietnam to Afghanistan*, Dr. Ronald Glaser, a former officer in the Army Medical Corps during Vietnam, detailed the primary reasons why more service members were surviving their wounds: twenty-first-century body armor made of advanced ceramics and Kevlar that protects the head, torso, and vital organs, and in some cases can stop an AK-47 round or the shrapnel of a grenade; advances in combat medicine and techniques, such as easy-to-use tourniquets, advanced blood-clotting medicines, and increased training for combat medics in treating hemorrhaging; in-theater Forward Surgical Teams focused on the single overriding task of stabilizing the wounded for transport; and especially a rapid aeromedical evacuation system that in extremis could fly wounded troops to the U.S. military hospital in Landstuhl, Germany, in hours, not days.

In his own nearly miraculous odyssey of survival, Kyle Carpenter would benefit from all of those advances in combat medicine. And yet at the culmination of a journey that passed through an army of caregivers and supporters, only Carpenter and his fellow severely wounded warriors could answer an all-important question: Saved for what?

In November 2010, the 2nd Battalion, 9th Marines had been in Afghanistan for four months, and already it seemed like an eternity. They were stationed in the town of Marja in Helmand Province, the heart of Taliban country. It was a harsh, flat landscape of agricultural fields crisscrossed by canals and mud-walled farmhouses on the edge of a vast desert. The insurgents used the wasteland as sanctuary to stage constant attacks that took a heavy toll on the 2/9 Marines. Late in September, Lance Corporal Timothy Jackson of Corbin, Kentucky, was killed by an improvised explosive device. Then Sergeant Zachary Stinson stepped on an IED and lost both legs above the knee. In early November, nineteen-year-old Dakota Huse of Greenwood, Louisiana, was killed when he similarly stepped on an IED while on patrol in Marja. Days later, Fox Company of the 2/9 was ordered to establish a new patrol base in the village to help pacify the Taliban stronghold. The Marines named it Patrol Base Dakota.

The walled compound they occupied consisted of a few two-story buildings, and within days a fortified outlook position on one of the roofs was hit and destroyed in a rocket attack. Corporal Kyle Carpenter had just come down from the roof and was inside the building at the time, but he somehow escaped with nothing more than a ringing in his ears. A few days later, insurgents crawled to within thirty yards of the compound using a weed-choked canal just outside its walls for cover, tossing three hand grenades into the courtyard. The explosions wounded Lance Corporals Bradley Skipper and Jacob Belote, who were both evacuated by helicopter.

With one of their buildings destroyed, the Marines used their remaining scarce sandbags to build an observation post atop a second building. On November 21, Carpenter and his best friend, Corporal Nicholas Eufrazio, were leaning back against the sandbags, taking occasional sniper fire and going through "what if" scenarios of what they would do if the Taliban attacked in force.

They were a study in contrasts—Carpenter, a churchgoing southern boy from small-town South Carolina, and Eufrazio a wisecracking kid from Plymouth, Massachusetts, who cursed like a sailor. But in the hellfire of Helmand they forged an unbreakable bond.

"So Nick, what happens if they throw a grenade up here?" Carpenter recalls asking his friend on that rooftop, as recounted in *You Are Worth It*.

"My ass is off this fucking roof," said Eufrazio.

"Dude, I'm right behind you," Carpenter replied with a laugh.

Not long afterward, something landed on the rooftop with a soft thud and puff of dust, and it was suddenly no laughing matter. Kyle Carpenter didn't jump off the roof. Rather, he lunged forward toward the grenade, disappearing into the blast cloud. When his squadmates reached the rooftop, Carpenter's shredded body was lying facedown directly over a blast hole that punched through the roof into the ceiling below, his body still smoldering.

Carpenter's helmet was riddled with shrapnel holes, and much of his gear had melted on his body from the intense heat of the blast. His rifle was mangled like a pretzel. An explosive ordnance disposal expert attached to the platoon would later testify to Medal of Honor investigators that the grenade had to have been covered by a heavy object to blast through the roof like that. By all appearances Carpenter threw himself on the grenade in order to save his friend Nick Eufrazio, who was also grievously wounded by shrapnel.

All Kyle Carpenter remembered is that his world suddenly disappeared into white static. Despite the fact that a portion of his face was hanging off his skull, and his body was shredded and covered in wounds, his eyes were still open and he was semiconscious. Christopher "Doc" Frend, a Marine corpsman, or combat medic, worked furiously to stanch his bleeding and give him a slim chance at survival. As he was being treated, Carpenter spoke as if from a great distance, asking if he was going to die, and telling his fellow Marines over and over again that he was sorry.

"Is Nick okay? Is Nick okay?" he kept asking.

Kyle Carpenter refused to give up or wallow in understandable self-pity, because he somehow found renewed purpose at the National Naval Medical Center in Bethesda. That positive attitude would have to sustain him through two and a half years in and out of the hospital and an excruciating rehabilitation that required that he learn to walk and tie his own shoes again. There were brain surgeries to remove shrapnel from his head and repair a collapsed lung, and nearly forty surgeries to repair his shattered right arm and fractured fingers. In time he acquired a new jaw and teeth and a prosthetic eye.

Carpenter found strength in his faith and the support of

his close family, especially his parents, Jim and Robin, who kept a nearly constant vigil at his bedside through months and years of recovery, and his twin younger brothers, Peyton and Price. He was determined to reward the efforts of the hundreds of medical professionals who helped piece him back together, and to keep faith with his Marine brothers by not letting his injuries and those who inflicted them define his life.

A football standout in high school, Kyle Carpenter eventually reclaimed an active life, skiing, snowboarding, and skydiving. He even completed the Marine Corps Marathon. He also went back to school and graduated college, and served as a Marine Corps ambassador and motivational speaker on behalf of his fellow wounded warriors. He became a social media sensation, with 436,000 Instagram followers and 50,000 on Twitter, where his handle is @chicksdigscars.

In 2014, Corporal Kyle Carpenter became the youngest living recipient of the Medal of Honor, the nation's highest award for valor, at just twenty-four years of age. At the ceremony, special note was made of the continuing struggles of the young Marine that Carpenter had tried to save. Lance Corporal Nick Eufrazio suffered a traumatic brain injury that day, and was still recovering from his own devastating wounds.

Carpenter's surprisingly generous memoir, *You Are Worth It*, cowritten with Don Yaeger, became a national bestseller. As it turned out, Carpenter put all that time in the hospital to good use contemplating the meaning of his life, and in the book's pages he is revealed as a warrior philosopher with a keen understanding of the universality of struggle.

"I wrote the book to help people. I wrote it to show people that you can come back better and stronger," Carpenter said in an interview with *Task & Purpose*. "You can make it and you can get through it. Not only can you get through it, but you can come out on the other side smiling."

In the memoir, Carpenter recalls that of all the many frightening hallucinations he endured on the long road to recovery, the one that he can't seem to shake is witnessing his own funeral. So he characteristically turned his worst nightmare into a positive motivator.

"I am still haunted by the feeling of emptiness and despair that I felt when I realized no one came," he writes. "I think every day about how I am using the life that my health-care team worked so hard to preserve for me. Am I touching people's lives in a meaningful way? Am I leaving a legacy that matters? What am I doing with my second shot at life?"

Chapter 19

—☆—

Immigrant, Soldier, Hero

Army Captain Florent A. Groberg

The brigade commander was in a late-night planning session, so security team leader Captain Florent Groberg poked his head into the office of Command Sergeant Major Kevin Griffin. As the senior noncommissioned officer for Task Force Mountain Warrior, Griffin served as a father figure to more than three thousand soldiers under his command in Afghanistan, and he was a pretty good argument for why the NCO corps is considered the backbone of the U.S. Army.

A newly minted captain, Florent Groberg never passed up an opportunity to stop by for a talk with the senior enlisted man. He considered Sergeant Major Griffin a mentor. The young officer and the seasoned NCO had formed an unlikely friendship, though in civilian life they might never have crossed paths. Army life in a time of war had a way of forging strong bonds and a sense of camaraderie among people even from wildly different backgrounds.

Groberg was an immigrant from France whose mother, Klara, was a French-Algerian Muslim. His adopted father, Larry Groberg, was an American and former Motorola Iridium executive who had been stationed in Paris. The elder Groberg lured his eleven-year-old adopted son to the United States with promises of McDonald's Happy Meals and a chance to see Michael Jordan play basketball.

A track star in high school and a runner on the track team

at the University of Maryland, "Flo" Groberg became a naturalized American citizen in 2001, the same year that Al Qaeda extremists attacked his adoptive country and killed nearly three thousand civilians. He had an immigrant's unshakable love of country, and the terrorist attacks kindled in him a burning desire for retribution. So in August 2012, Groberg was four years into his Army career and already on his second combat deployment, still learning the ropes of what he considered the world's most important and rewarding profession—leading troops in combat.

By contrast, Griffin was a burly forty-five-year-old Army veteran and father of two from the small town of Riverton, Wyoming. A state wrestling champion at Riverton High, he had devoted his entire adult life and twenty-four years to the U.S. Army. Already on his fifth combat deployment, he had long since mastered the art of keeping his troops both in line and loose with a combination of discipline and laughter. He could spot a uniform violation a mile away, and then offer to buy a round of tequila shots when they all returned safely back home. There wasn't a U.S. outpost or forward operating base in Kunar Province too remote for Griffin to visit and dispense his critiques and jokes, weighted as the situation demanded. Mostly he just loved the Army and those he judged sufficiently dedicated to it, and his soldiers repaid the sentiment in kind. Already his son and nephew had followed Sergeant Major Kevin Griffin into the family business of soldiering, as so often happens.

Despite the vast difference in their ages and backgrounds,

Groberg and Griffin found much to discuss in their late-night talks, usually as they waited for Colonel James Mingus, commander of their 4th Brigade Combat Team, 4th Infantry Division, to finish for the day and dismiss them. On the eve of their deployment, Captain Flo Groberg had promised Mingus's wife that he would bring her husband home safe, and as the security team leader he shadowed the colonel nearly every waking hour. He meant to keep his promise.

In their talks Griffin told stories of his life growing up in Wyoming, and of his wife, Pam, and their two children. He also shared insights from his previous combat deployments. For his part, Groberg revealed that when he was a boy one of his favorite uncles, a soldier in the Algerian army, had been murdered and beheaded by the GIA Islamist extremist group, his body sent to his maternal grandfather as a warning. The family was never quite the same after that atrocity, and his mother took the death of her brother especially hard. All of Flo Groberg's life seemed to have been building toward a fight with these extremists who murdered so wantonly.

Of course the main topic of conversation in the late-night talks between Groberg and Griffin was the situation in the task force's area of operations in remote Kunar Province. A region in the far northeastern corner of Afghanistan where the Kunar River flowed down the mountains and spilled into a basin of fertile farmland, Kunar was a land of infinite beauty and menace. It was part of the Regional Command East (RC East), where the U.S. military made its last major offensive push of the war. In that sense RC East was where America's longest war—already ten-plus years and counting in 2012—had come full circle.

Just across the border and the invisible Durand Line that has separated Afghanistan and Pakistan since British colonial days, CIA operatives once armed the mujahedeen who fought the Soviet army. Some of those Islamist guerrilla fighters later formed Al Qaeda and joined the Taliban. By the summer of 2012, it was the U.S.-led coalition that was in the process of withdrawing thirty thousand troops from Afghanistan and handing operations over to the struggling Afghan security forces. The Afghan troops were gaining the upper hand in larger population centers such as the provincial capital of Asadabad, but a Taliban assassination and intimidation campaign had cowed local leaders and the inhabitants of remote mountain villages in the region. The government controlled the urban population centers, but the insurgency ruled much of the countryside.

That dynamic suggested a twilight struggle that neither side was likely to win or lose, especially as long as the Taliban and affiliated extremist groups found sanctuary in Pakistan's wild tribal regions. In the meantime, the plan was for all U.S. and NATO combat units to withdraw from the country by 2014. The border region of RC East was where the U.S. war in Afghanistan began, with Osama bin Laden and his Al Qaeda lieutenants retreating into Pakistan from the caves of Tora Bora. For better or worse, it was likely to end there.

★ ★ ★

As the Black Hawk helicopters touched down in a cloud of dust at Forward Operating Base Fiaz on August 8, 2012, Captain Florent Groberg already had a bad feeling about the mission. The night before, he had made a courtesy call to FOB Fiaz to alert them that a delegation of senior leaders would be visiting the next day. The high-level group included two brigade commanders, two battalion commanders, the brigade command sergeant major, a battalion command sergeant major, and an Afghan National Army battalion commander. Groberg asked for a standard fifteen-man security team to escort the group by foot to a scheduled meeting at the provincial governor's compound in Asadabad. The major in charge at FOB Fiaz told him that a security detail wouldn't be necessary, and members of his unit would scout the route in advance and meet the delegation at the governor's compound. Dumbfounded, Groberg assumed that the man would come to his senses when he read the roster of high-level officers.

But when the helicopter rotors quieted and the dust settled at FOB Fiaz the next morning, Groberg realized there really would be no local security detail. He scrambled to assemble a diamond-shaped formation, with the VIPs in the rear and his six-man security team on the edges, even drafting a local cook from FOB Fiaz to join in protecting the formation. Groberg moved from his customary spot in the back with Colonel Mingus and took the point instead. He had been on numerous missions and scores of engagements with the enemy, and he recognized wrong when he saw it. Everything about this shorthanded movement through the dusty streets of Asad-abad felt slapdash and off-kilter.

As they walked outside the wire, the group followed a route skirting the Kunar River, and then veered toward the center of town along a street of cinderblock buildings. As they rounded a curve in the road, Groberg came to a bridge across a muddy canal. The formation halted as two Afghans on small motorcycles began to cross the bridge from the other side. An Afghan Army officer walking point alongside Groberg shouted at the motorcyclists in Pashto, gesturing for them to turn around. Then a strange thing happened. The two riders dumped their bikes on the bridge and started running away in the opposite direction.

Captain Groberg's head was immediately on a swivel. There were a number of pedestrians milling around on the streets, but an Afghan man exiting a compound on the left caught his eye. The man was walking in their direction, backward.

Groberg shouted at the man to stop, but the Afghan kept approaching. So Groberg ran up and shoved the man in the chest with the butt of his M16 rifle. He felt the suicide vest underneath his flowing clothes, and then pushed the Afghan away from the formation in a bum's rush. He felt rather than saw Sergeant Andrew Mahoney join the grappling match and help push the insurgent farther away from the formation, wrestling him to the ground. Neither of them saw the "dead man's trigger" that engaged as soon as the suicide bomber relaxed his grip.

* * *

When he regained consciousness, Groberg was propped up on his body armor in the middle of the street, a scene of chaos unspooling before him as if in slow motion. He stared in shock at his leg. The fibula bone was sticking out grotesquely and his foot faced backward at an impossible angle. He tried to drag himself up but couldn't. Checking for internal injuries, he saw that his body was covered in blood and bone fragments. Then he remembered the suicide bomber.

Sergeant First Class Brian Brink grabbed Groberg by his webbing and dragged him to cover. Despite being wounded in the blast, Specialist Daniel Balderrama, the team's combat medic, hurriedly wrapped a tourniquet around Groberg's leg to stop the bleeding, and then tried to keep him from lapsing into a coma. They were moving so fast, yet everything seemed to be happening in slow motion for Groberg. Then he remembered why he was there.

"Did he get Colonel Mingus?" Groberg asked.

As it turned out, the explosion of the first bomber's vest ignited the explosives of a second suicide bomber who was hiding nearby next to the road. The quick reaction of Captain Groberg and Sergeant Mahoney had kept the suicide bombers away from the formation and saved the lives of many of the senior officers. Nearby, Colonel Mingus was crouched behind a chest-high wall applying a tourniquet to the arm of Sergeant Mahoney, who had also been severely wounded in the explosion.

"No, Mingus is alive," Balderrama said. "But they killed Sergeant Major Griffin."

"Show me! Take me to Sergeant Major Griffin," Groberg ordered his men.

The soldiers carried him over to the bodies of his slain teammates. He saw Major Tom Kennedy, a West Pointer who loved hockey and was a role model to younger officers because of the genuine concern he always showed for his troops. Beside him was Air Force Major David Gray, another popular officer with a quick smile and friends wherever he went. Foreign service officer Ragaei Abdelfattah, an Egyptian immigrant who worked for the U.S. Agency for International Development, had also been killed. And beside him lay Command Sergeant Major Kevin Griffin, the mentor who had always made time for Groberg when the young officer felt like talking. All of them gone in a flash on the worst day of Florent Groberg's life.

Staring at their bodies, Groberg was overwhelmed with grief and rage. Somehow he had failed them all. Then he noticed an Afghan man standing near the bodies and smiling at the carnage. *Smiling!* Without hesitating, he reached for a nearby weapon with the intent of shooting the son of a bitch dead. Someone grabbed his arm and stayed it. Groberg looked into the youthful face of Private First Class Eric Ochart, who had obviously read his intentions.

"It's not worth it, sir," said Ochart, part of a team that had saved Flo Groberg's life not once, but now twice in just a matter of minutes. A few minutes that would shape his life forever.

★ ★ ★

Months later, Groberg found himself wide awake in the middle of the night. The demons unleashed by survivor's guilt were swirling around Room 401 at Walter Reed National Military Medical Center, feeding off his excruciating physical and emotional pain and slowly eating him alive. The left leg with half the calf muscle blown away was swathed in bandages, a vacuum tube rhythmically sucking blood out of the wound. His right leg was encased in a tight sleeve to keep his blood circulating. The college track star who once dreamed of running in the Olympics was now seriously considering having his leg amputated.

Groberg's head was constantly ringing from the ruptured eardrum that left him legally deaf in the left ear. The traumatic brain injury he had suffered caused bewildering memory lapses, rendering him unable to calculate how many quarters were in a dollar, or recall the name "giraffe" when shown a drawing of the animal. Meanwhile, it was 3:30 a.m., and every fifteen minutes he jabbed a button for another shot of morphine. Stimulated by the narcotic, the demons went into a new feeding frenzy of recrimination.

"You failed them! You let your team down! You didn't do your job! Why are you alive? Why are your friends dead? It's all your fault! You don't deserve to live!"

Finally the morphine brought merciful unconsciousness, and then a bright light and sharp noise snatched Groberg awake and back into an unbearable reality. A first-year resident doctor was asking how he was sleeping. The clock read 4 a.m.

"Get the hell out of my room!" Groberg screamed.

By the time the long wars in Afghanistan and Iraq approached and then passed the decade mark, the physical and mental wounds had amassed into something like a pathology unique to these conflicts, albeit one that mutated over time. As the conflicts dragged on, with tactics, equipment, and geography shifting over the years, the profile of wounds also changed. Early on in Afghanistan small arms caused most of the injuries. Then a few years into the fighting in Iraq—as improvised explosive devices got bigger and the armor on U.S. military vehicles thicker—troops absorbed blast waves through their seats, causing a spike in spinal cord injuries, concussions, and brain trauma. By 2012, Afghanistan had become a war of dismounted infantry, and the polytrauma wards of military hospitals were almost overwhelmed by an influx of troopers with massive injuries from absorbing blasts.

According to the advocacy group Veterans for Common Sense, by 2012 more than 190,000 veterans of Iraq and Afghanistan had suffered a concussion or brain injury. The Pentagon judged 160,000 wounded warriors from the conflicts as "60 percent disabled" or higher. There was also growing evidence of links between traumatic brain injury and posttraumatic stress disorder (PTSD), with both affecting similar areas of the brain and exhibiting similar symptoms. A Rand Corporation survey found that one in five veterans of Iraq and

Afghanistan—some 300,000 people by 2012—were suffering either from major depression or PTSD, while 320,000 suffered from concussions or traumatic brain injury.

And then there was the honor roll of nearly 7,000 fallen service members from Afghanistan and Iraq. The shock of their loss continues to reverberate across a landscape of grief inhabited not only by their families, but also by their former comrades in arms, many of whom suffer acute attacks of survivor's guilt.

At Florent Groberg's lowest point at Walter Reed he was rescued by a guardian angel by the name of Staff Sergeant Travis Mills. Earlier in the year Mills had been critically injured by an IED on his third tour in Afghanistan, losing portions of both legs and both arms. He was one of only five quadruple amputees from the wars in Afghanistan and Iraq to survive such massive injuries. Even as he struggled with his own catastrophic wounds, Mills heard from the Walter Reed medical staff that there was a very angry captain in Room 401 who was pissed off at the world. So he stopped by to help and try to provide some perspective.

"Travis Mills basically told me, 'Listen, man, I know what you're going through is terrible, but there are a lot of people here who are also going through tough days,'" Groberg recalled in an interview with the author. "He told me that I would have many opportunities to still make a difference with my life, and that I had a responsibility to my soldiers and those that I had lost to tell their stories and remember the positive things they did." So in just fifteen minutes he completely changed my perspective. He helped me rediscover my inner warrior. I started thinking like a soldier again, with a mission and sense of purpose. At a time when I was in danger of giving up on myself, Travis Mills showed me the light."

In 2015, Travis Mills's faith that his fellow wounded warrior could still make a difference with his life was rewarded when Captain Florent Groberg was awarded the Medal of Honor during a ceremony in the East Room of the White House. The entire team who shared the worst day of his life reunited to celebrate one of the best, along with the Gold Star families of the fallen, whose names Groberg still wears on a bracelet. He would go on to coauthor an excellent memoir of his experiences, entitled *8 Seconds of Courage: A Soldier's Story from Immigrant to the Medal of Honor.*

"The Medal of Honor is an unbelievable honor, but also a burden, because I feel a responsibility to earn it every day, and to try and make a difference in other people's lives," Groberg said in our interview. "To be honest, I don't even consider it my medal. I'm just a courier carrying the story of everyone in my unit, and especially those that didn't make it home."

Chapter 20

Shadow Warriors

Navy Chief (SEAL) Edward C. Byers Jr.

By 2012, the Navy's SEAL Team 6 had become one of the most renowned and lethally efficient special operations strike forces in history. Driven by a relentless cycle of operations and intelligence exploitation that Joint Special Operations Command dubbed "F3EA"—Find-Fix-Finish-Exploit-Analyze— SEAL Team 6 and its Army counterpart Delta Force had been executing capture-or-kill night raids in Afghanistan and Iraq for a decade, sometimes dozens in a single night. Some of the U.S. commandos had hundreds of raids under their belts, far exceeding the experience level achieved by special operations counterparts during the Vietnam War or even World War II.

Driven by the imperative for surprise and stealth in their classified "black operations," the SEALs lived a creed of working in the shadows: "I do not advertise the nature of my work, nor seek recognition for my actions."

Yet even their pledge of secrecy could not ward off the publicity that surrounded two of SEAL Team 6's most daring operations. In 2009 the unit rescued American merchant marine captain Richard Phillips, who was being held at sea by Somali pirates. After a daring high-altitude low-opening (HALO) parachute jump over open ocean at night, SEAL Team snipers killed three of the pirates and successfully rescued Phillips.

Most famously, in 2011 Seal Team 6 conducted Operation Neptune Spear, flying deep into hostile territory in Pakistan on the night raid that killed archterrorist Osama bin Laden, finally avenging Al Qaeda's September 11, 2001, attacks on the United States.

That thirst for action and the riskiest missions came at a steep cost. Many of the SEAL Team commandos had logged combat deployments in the double digits. The personal upheaval and time away from home put tremendous stress on the families of special operators, as did the inability of team members to discuss with loved ones exactly what they did for a living. There was also the burden of grief and loss that weighed heavily on the elite units and the families that supported them: Since 9/11, seventy members of the small, tight-knit Naval Special Warfare community had made the ultimate sacrifice.

★ ★ ★

Looking back, SEAL chief Edward Byers Jr. seemed destined to serve. Even as a young kid and Boy Scout growing up in Grand Rapids, Ohio, he reveled in playing military games in the woods with his friends. After playing varsity soccer and graduating from Otsego High School he joined the Navy, following in the footsteps of his father, a Navy veteran of World War II who was buried in Arlington Cemetery.

Byers began his Navy career as a hospital corpsman, or medic, but ever since viewing a movie about the SEALs growing up he had dreamed of one day joining their ranks. He passed the grueling Basic Underwater Demolition/SEAL

(BUD/S) training in 2002, joining the roughly 25 percent of his class that made the grade. In December 2012, he was thirty-three years old, and already on his eleventh overseas deployment and ninth combat tour. He had received five Bronze Star medals for valor, and two Purple Hearts for wounds suffered in action, and still he cherished the life of a special warfare operator. He got to perform the work he loved alongside men he considered the toughest and most resilient on the planet.

On the night of December 8, 2012, Chief Ed Byers was bouncing in the webbed seat of a CH-47 Chinook helicopter as it hurtled over the mountains of eastern Afghanistan. He and the rest of the SEAL team assaulters had volunteered for the operation, fully aware that hostage rescue missions were considered "no fail" and thus among the riskiest. Whatever dangers they encountered, the rescuers were determined to bring an American hostage home alive.

So much depended on the accuracy of the intelligence. The hostage rescue team knew that Dr. Dilip Joseph was an American physician working for a nongovernmental organization that was trying to bring health care to remote Afghan villages. Three days earlier Dr. Joseph had been driving down a rural road en route from a medical clinic with two Afghan colleagues when their car was stopped by four armed men carrying AK-47 rifles. The insurgents tied their hands and threw them into the back of a truck, and then drove them to a remote mountain valley in Laghman Province in eastern Afghanistan. The two Afghan prisoners were later released, but JSOC intercepted intelligence that a Taliban commander was on his way to the compound where the American was being held, and planned to move him into Pakistan. At that point the odds were overwhelming that Dr. Joseph would never return to his wife and four children.

There was thus little time for rehearsal or careful planning, but the intelligence planners had a good bead on the target compound. The Chinook helicopters, piloted by members of the Army's elite 160th Special Operations Aviation Regiment, the famed Night Stalkers, landed near a mountain path, deposited the SEAL Team 6 rescue force, and then banked up into the inky blackness. Stamping in the bone-chilling cold, the SEAL commandos adjusted their packs and their night-vision goggles, and then set out on a nearly four-hour hike through the rugged mountains.

Finally the rescuers sighted the small, single-room target building, and they positioned themselves for the assault. Each team member knew his role in the deadly choreography to come, but a fight to rescue a hostage from armed guards at night in close quarters was by definition improvisational. Everything now depended on surprise, speed, and aggressive action on the target. Any misstep or hesitation could prove fatal.

The SEAL commandos crept to no more than seventy-five feet or so from the building's blanketed entrance, the landscape awash in the liquid green light of their night-vision goggles. Petty Officer First Class Nicolas "Nic" Checque took point, followed closely by Byers, who as the primary breacher was responsible for clearing the entrance to open a path for the rescue team. But before they could execute a surprise entry a guard came through the blankets, saw the Americans, and started to duck back inside.

Nic Checque immediately ran forward, firing his weapon at the guard, with Byers right on his heels. At the entrance Byers started to rip down the six blankets blocking the doorway, which were securely fastened to the wall and ceiling of the building. Aware that seconds could determine the captive's fate, Petty Officer Checque pushed through the blankets and was immediately cut down just inside the entranceway by a burst from an AK-47 rifle.

At the sound of gunfire, Chief Byers pushed his way into the dark room on the heels of his fallen friend, and in a single motion scanned the backside wall of the room and sighted and shot an insurgent aiming an AK-47 in his direction. In that moment he knew there was no time to think, it was react or be killed. Someone darted across the room and Byers lunged forward and tackled the man, not sure if he was friend or foe. He straddled the flailing stranger and pinned him down with his knees while using his other hand to adjust his night-vision goggles, which had been knocked askew in the struggle. He needed facial recognition to confirm that the man was not the American hostage.

"Dr. Joseph!" he called out. "Dr. Joseph!"

"I'm right here!" someone shouted in English not five feet away to the right.

Byers killed the Taliban fighter under his knees, and then leapt on top of Dr. Joseph to shield him with his body armor.

There was gunfire and the darkened room was dissected by sweeping searchlights on the weapons of SEAL commandos as they entered the room and looked for targets. Still shielding Joseph, Byers saw another armed Taliban within arm's reach and pinned the man to the wall by his throat. He held the man long enough for a teammate to take accurate aim and neutralize him with a kill shot. Byers still used his body to shield Dr. Joseph as the room suddenly grew quiet.

"Hey, are you okay? Are you hurt?" Byers asked the hostage. "You're safe now. You're with American forces."

In the three days since his capture, Dr. Dilip Joseph had been absolutely certain that he was going to die. Some of the Taliban fighters had taunted him by insisting that his fellow Americans would never come for him in such a remote and dangerous place. It turned out they were wrong.

"Yes, I'm okay. I'm fine," Joseph told his rescuer.

Chief Byers assisted Joseph outside the house and toward the helicopter landing zone, and then noticed a SEAL team medic working to stabilize Petty Officer Checque. As a medic himself, Byers ran over to assist. Checque was in bad shape, shot in the head at close range. During the entire forty-minute helicopter ride back to the hospital at Bagram Air Base, Chief Byers and other corpsmen performed CPR on the young SEAL commando from Monroeville, Pennsylvania, a stellar athlete who had played football and wrestled in high school, and had also dreamed as a young teenager of becoming a member of the elite SEALs.

At Bagram, the doctors pronounced twenty-eight-year-old

special warfare operator Nicolas Checque dead. For his heroism that night in laying down his life to rescue a fellow American he had never met, Nic Checque would posthumously receive the Navy Cross, the service's second-highest award for valor.

"Nic embodied what it was to be an American hero," Ed Byers said. "He will forever be remembered in the pages of history for the sacrifices that he made."

* * *

Three years after the rescue mission, Ed Byers received a phone call from the White House asking whether he would take a call from the president of the United States. He wondered out loud whether anyone ever actually said no to such a question. When President Barack Obama informed Byers that he would receive the Medal of Honor, he felt honored but also humbled. It was a weighty responsibility to represent the Naval Special Warfare community and stand in for all his brothers in arms who never made it home from war. Heroic men like Nic Checque, and so many like him.

That night Byers called his mother, Peggy, and told her about the news and the upcoming awards ceremony at the White House.

"Do you think I will be able to come?" she asked.

There was a pause on the other end of the line as Ed Byers suppressed a smile.

"Of course, Mom. I'm pretty sure you'll be allowed to come," he told her.

After his Medal of Honor ceremony, SEAL chief Ed Byers was eager to return to duty and the work he loved. So when the spotlight surrounding the award dimmed, he traded his starched dress blues for the familiar camouflage uniform and slipped back into the shadows of anonymity where courageous volunteers fight so that their countrymen can sleep peacefully at night.

Chapter 21

Last Man Out

Army Sergeant First Class
Thomas Patrick Payne

The back ramp of the CH-47 Chinook helicopter dropped and the U.S. and Kurdish special forces commandos rushed out into a swirling vortex of sand and rotor wash. Even with night-vision goggles they moved blindly at first, and immediately began taking machine-gun fire from the nearby prison complex. As rehearsed, the commandos quickly split into two assault groups to attack separate buildings where the terrorists of the Islamic State of Iraq and Syria (ISIS) were holding more than seventy hostages.

In a hostage rescue mission success depends on surprise and speed, and the first assault team was momentarily slowed and then nearly pinned down by interlocking fields of enemy fire. They were in danger of losing the initiative on which everything depended. Sensing hesitation, Master Sergeant Joshua Wheeler looked back at his team and motioned forward.

"On me!" he shouted.

The commandos fired and moved forward, fired and moved forward. Then Wheeler was felled and killed by enemy fire. Colleagues rushed to his side, and for critical seconds the assault's momentum seemed to waver.

In the second assault group, assistant team leader Sergeant First Class Patrick Payne, an Army Ranger assigned to Special Operations Command, heard the "man down" call over the radio, and immediately dispatched his medic to render aid.

The Kurdish fighters in his attack cell seemed disheartened by the quick news of casualties. Then another American commando stepped forward, swept his arm around the group, and pointed for them to look him in the eyes.

"Follow me!" he shouted, and then moved forward.

Sergeant Payne's team met only light resistance at their objective, and they quickly cut the lock on the prison door and freed nearly forty hostages. The expressions of joy and surprise on the faces of the Iraqi prisoners, many of whom were crying from relief as they were liberated, were a sight the Americans would never forget. But Payne and his team couldn't get caught up in the exhilaration of the moment. They still had a job to do.

The sounds of a firefight at the first objective only thirty or forty yards away grew steadily louder. At that moment Payne received the call for help over the radio that would change his life. He looked at his teammate and nodded toward the deafening sound of gunfire.

"Let's get into the fight," was all Payne said.

For good reasons, hostage rescue missions have an almost mythic status in the lore of special forces worldwide. Successfully rescuing prisoners from a determined enemy requires airtight intelligence, extreme tactical proficiency, and bravado, plus speed, stealth, and not a little luck. And the stakes are always life and death.

For instance, the 1976 raid on Entebbe by Israeli commandos, who freed more than one hundred Jewish hostages from
Palestinian terrorists in hostile territory in Uganda, solidi-
fied the world-class reputation of the Israel Defense Forces.
By contrast, the failure of the Army's elite Delta Force to
rescue American hostages held by Iran in 1980's Operation
Eagle Claw was a blow to the prestige of the U.S. military, and
was a major factor in the creation of the unified U.S. Special
Operations Command (SOCOM) in 1987. From SOCOM's
inception, hostage rescue was thus a top training and mission
priority and deeply embedded in the command's culture.

When the Joint Special Operations Task Force in Iraq
supporting Operation Inherent Resolve was approached by
the Kurdistan Regional Government in October 2015, task
force members immediately grasped the urgency of the mission. Intelligence photos revealed recently dug mass graves
at a prison in the northern Iraqi town of Hawija, where the
brutal terrorists of ISIS were holding more than seventy Iraqi
hostages. Just the year before ISIS fighters had massacred an
estimated seventeen hundred captured Iraqi Army cadets and
militiamen at Camp Speicher near Tikrit, machine-gunning
them into ditches and freshly dug graves in one of the deadliest acts of mass murder in modern history. The atrocity was
an early indication that ISIS was determined to make barbar-
ity its brand.

"In combat you are constantly studying the enemy, and
the enemy is constantly studying you, but conducting a hostage rescue mission behind enemy lines at night is something

we prepare to do every single day at Special Operations Command," said Sergeant Major Payne in an interview with the author. They start planning hostage rescue missions from the simple conviction, he said, that failure is not an option.

"When the Kurdish government reached out for our assistance in a hostage rescue mission, we all considered it a 'no fail' mission. We were not going to fail our partners," said Payne in the interview. "We knew it was highly probable that those hostages would be executed if we didn't action that target. And we considered it our duty to bring those people home."

The radio call for help at a critical moment in the mission triggered a profound determination in then–First Sergeant Payne.

"The moment that was most important to me in that fight was that call of a teammate in need," he said. "This was a man I knew, and a great teammate, and it was understood that we would be there for each other, and for our partners. That moment was when I hit another warfighting gear that I didn't know I had."

The second prison building holding hostages was already on fire when Payne and another U.S. commando approached in the night. ISIS fighters were barricaded inside, holding the assault team off with constant machine-gun fire. The rescue team was also taking fire from an ISIS position off to the west.

Payne and his colleague climbed a ladder to the roof of

the building, looking for another way in. They tossed grenades and fired into the barricaded windows and door below to try and silence the machine gun, to no avail. Then Payne heard screams of "Allahu akbar!" from inside the building, and felt as much as heard the explosion of suicide vests. The rooftop shook and the building teetered on the verge of collapse.

Back on the ground, Payne and members of his team tried to breach the building's fortified walls and windows, but several of the Kurdish commandos were hit by enemy fire in the attempt, forcing them all back. Fire and smoke poured from the building. Time was running out for the hostages.

Near the front entryway where several Kurdish commandos had already been wounded, Payne was able to see inside to a hallway. The main prison door had the same type of lock that he had broken through in the first building. And Payne still had the bolt cutters on him.

"What do you got?" his sergeant major asked, appearing at his side.

"Sergeant Major, I got the same prison door as the one in the building I just liberated!"

"Okay, I got it!" the sergeant major said in the shorthand understood by commandos in action.

Payne knew that meant the sergeant major had his back. As the man moved into position next to the entryway to lay down covering fire against the ISIS fighters barricaded in the back, Payne gripped the bolt cutters tightly. Then he ran into the burning building to the sound of gunfire and bullet impacts all around.

* * *

For a boy who grew up near an Army base in the small South Carolina town of Batesburg-Leesville, a life in the military seemed a natural and noble idea. Payne's grandfather was an Army veteran who fought in World War II, Korea, and Vietnam. His father, a police officer, would take the young Payne to Fort Jackson on the Fourth of July to let him play among the tanks and helicopters on display and talk to the veterans who gathered there. Both of Payne's brothers, not to mention his cousins and many of his high school friends, signed up for military service.

"It was pretty special being from a small town, where we kind of drew inspiration from our veteran community," said Payne. "Those old-timers kind of built us up as young men, and gave us a solid foundation to grow on."

Payne was a senior in high school when the nation was attacked on September 11, 2001, and that sealed the deal. He enlisted in the Army soon after, and though he was slight in stature and only about 120 pounds soaking wet at the time, he applied for and passed the Ranger Assessment and Selection Program, and was eventually assigned to the elite 75th Ranger Regiment. His career in U.S. Special Forces had begun.

It almost ended when Payne was wounded in combat in Afghanistan in 2010, a grenade blast shattering his knee. The wound built up so much scar tissue that eventually he could no longer bend his knee properly, and an Army doctor told him that he might have to choose another career. Then, during that summer of recuperation, he met his future wife, Alison, a two-sport athlete in college who would later become a nurse. That was all the inspiration he needed. Their first date was a run along the dam at Lake Murray, South Carolina.

Improbably, less than two years after being wounded in action, Payne was part of a two-man team representing U.S. Special Operations Command in the grueling Best Ranger Competition, which they won.

"We had the opportunity and we capitalized on it during that competition, and were able to bring home the Gold Cup to Special Operations Command," said Payne, who described his actions on October 22, 2015, in remarkably similar terms: an opportunity seized and acted on.

Payne was coughing and nearly overcome by smoke inhalation when he staggered out of the burning prison building. He had managed to cut the first lock on the prison door and narrowly avoid being shot, but he couldn't breathe inside the inferno. Once outside, he handed the bolt cutters to a Kurdish commando, who tried unsuccessfully to cut the second lock before retreating from the building.

With only minutes to spare before the hostages would be burned alive, Payne seized the bolt cutters and once again ran into the burning building. The cloud of noxious fumes inside had dropped to below his waist, and the acrid smoke burned in his lungs. Yet somehow in an adrenaline-fueled rush he found the strength to cut the second lock and kick the door open.

The hostages inside were coughing and weeping, many of them disoriented and too afraid to move in the midst of so much gunfire. Payne forcefully directed the group to the entryway, physically grabbing and pulling some of them toward the doorway as enemy fire tore through the walls from the rear of the building. Outside, his teammates created a human wall, standing shoulder to shoulder and using their body armor and risking their own lives to shield the hostages from ISIS fire as they stumbled out of the building.

Payne entered the burning building two more times to guide the last disoriented hostages to safety, ISIS fighters still firing from their barricaded positions in the rear of the prison. He appeared in the smoke-filled doorway a final time, and then issued the call that everyone on the raid was anxiously waiting to hear.

"Last man out!" shouted Payne.

On September 11, 2020, aptly on the anniversary of the 9/11 attacks that launched the United States' global war against terrorists, then–Sergeant Major Thomas "Patrick" Payne traveled to the White House to receive the Medal of Honor from President Donald J. Trump, the nation's highest award for valor bestowed for his part in one of the largest hostage rescues in history.

Over nearly a score of combat deployments, Sergeant Major Payne had fought on virtually every front in the United States' global war against terrorists and extremists. He insists that his actions at the prison compound on October 22, 2015, were just what all of his teammates expected of each other.

"Every man on the mission that night was engaged in their own unique problem set. My teammates were also looking for some way to liberate those hostages," said Payne. "I just happened to be the man at the right place with the bolt cutters. So I had to find a way to capitalize on the opportunity that I was given."

Yet especially for special operations forces, there is something about hostage rescue missions that speak to the ethos of the organization. In that sense the Hawija prison raid that successfully rescued more than seventy people from the grip of would-be ISIS executioners rightfully takes its place in the mythic lore of the profession.

"It was an honor for me to participate that night, because you live for hostage rescues," said Payne. "When you look back on that night, it embodies the selfless service of my teammates. Especially Sergeant Joshua Wheeler. They put the lives of the hostages above their own. When you think about Army values like duty, personal courage, and selfless service, that's what stands out to me about that mission."

Payne thinks often about the sacrifice inherent in those values and that level of commitment, and for good reason. When his and Alison's second son was born, they named him Josh in memory of a fallen comrade.

About the Author

James Kitfield is currently a Senior Fellow and Journalist-in-Residence at the Center for the Study of the Presidency & Congress, and former senior national security correspondent for the Atlantic Media Company and *National Journal*. Mr. Kitfield's articles on defense, national security, intelligence, and foreign policy issues have appeared in numerous print and online sources, among them the *New York Times, Washington Post, Atlantic, POLITICO Magazine, National Journal,* and *Yahoo News*. He is the only three-time recipient of the prestigious Gerald R. Ford Award for Distinguished Reporting on National Defense, most recently for his first-hand reporting on the Afghan War. The Military Reporters and Editors Association (MRE) and the Medill School of Journalism have awarded Mr. Kitfield their top prize for excellence in reporting an unprecedented six times, and the National Press Club has honored him with its Edwin Hood Award for Diplomatic Correspondence. Mr. Kitfield is the author of three books, most recently *Twilight Warriors: The Soldiers, Spies & Special Agents Who Are Revolutionizing the American Way of War*. He lives in Alexandria, VA.